# The SHARP™ Method

# The SHARP™ Method

Strategic Holistic Accelerated Recovery Program

How to Maximize Your Surgical Recovery
With Functional & Traditional Medicine

Written by

Dr. Robert Whitfield, MD

Foreword by JJ Virgin

ISBN: 979-8-89316-804-4 - eBook
ISBN: 979-8-89316-805-1 - Paperback

*This book is in memory of my mother, father, and sister, who passed away in that order. My brother and I are left to carry on their memory. Everything I do is for Ashley, Heath, and Vivian. In the end, all you have is family.*

# CONTENTS

# FOREWORD

When it comes to transformation—whether it's related to our health, appearance, or even our mindset—there's a tendency to focus on the "big moment." It could be the day you decide to make a lifestyle change, the morning of a significant surgery, or the instant you commit to a new health regimen. However, the journey itself often gets overlooked, especially the crucial phases of preparation and recovery.

Throughout my career as a nutrition and fitness expert, I've had the privilege of working closely with plastic surgeons, offering my services and guidance to their patients. Over the years, I've gained a unique insider's perspective on the world of cosmetic and reconstructive surgery. And what I've seen has been both eye-opening and, quite frankly, troubling.

The standard approach to surgery has typically been narrowly focused on the procedure itself: the physical act of cutting, reshaping, and repairing the body. The assumption has been that once the surgeon has done their job, the hard part is over. But as any patient who has undergone a major operation can attest, the true challenge lies in the recovery process.

All too often, patients are sent home with little more than a list of dos and don'ts and left to navigate the often-grueling road to healing on their own. Nutrition, supplementation, stress management, and other critical recovery considerations are routinely overlooked despite their profound impact on outcomes.

Worse yet, many patients are actively discouraged from taking a proactive approach to their healing. I still vividly remember a conversation with a plastic surgeon who expressed his disinterest in the post-surgery follow-up. His indifference wasn't due to a lack of care but rather a feeling of helplessness: there was nothing he felt he could offer his patients to facilitate their healing process.

It was a sobering realization that some of the medical professionals entrusted with our care viewed the recovery process as a low priority rather than an integral part of the surgical journey. And that simply wasn't good enough, not in my book.

That's why I was so profoundly impressed when I first met Dr. Robert Whitfield and learned about his revolutionary SHARP protocol. Short for "Strategic Holistic Accelerated Recovery Program," SHARP represents a seismic shift in how we approach surgical recovery. I've had the pleasure of knowing Dr. Rob for two years, and he continues to inspire me.

Rather than viewing recovery as an afterthought, Dr. Rob has elevated it to the center of his practice, crafting a comprehensive, integrative model that addresses every phase of the surgical experience.

Dr. Rob understands something that far too many of his colleagues have missed: surgery is not just a singular event but rather a profound physiological and psychological journey that requires meticulous preparation and support, both before and after the procedure. It's not just about the results, which in themselves are transformative, but about the journey. It's smoother, quicker, and more complete, embodying a level of care that goes beyond the norm. He is doing something genuinely transformational in an area that has long been neglected. From the moment a patient walks through his doors, he is laser-focused on optimizing their body, mind, and spirit for the challenges that lie ahead.

It starts with a deep dive into the patient's genetic profile, using cutting-edge testing to identify any imbalances or dysfunctions that could impede the healing process. Based on those insights, Dr. Rob then crafts a customized supplement regimen, using a strategic blend of vitamins, minerals, and other targeted nutrients to address those root causes.

Dr. Rob also conducts a comprehensive toxicity assessment, identifying and mitigating environmental factors that could sabotage the patient's health. From heavy metals and mold exposure to endocrine-disrupting chemicals, he leaves no potential culprit unchecked.

With that foundational work complete, the focus shifts to diet, nutrition, and gut health—the cornerstones of a robust immune system and efficient inflammatory response. Dr. Rob works closely with each patient to craft a nutrition plan that is not only delicious and satisfying but scientifically calibrated to support the body's natural healing mechanisms.

Of course, hormones play a critical role in the recovery process as well, especially for female patients. That's why Dr. Rob takes a deep dive into each person's hormonal profile, using targeted interventions to ensure optimal balance and metabolic efficiency.

However, what truly sets SHARP apart is the way it bridges the gap between pre-operative preparation and post-operative recovery. Rather than viewing the surgical event as a discrete moment in time, Dr. Rob sees it as the centerpiece of a seamless, holistic process.

The moment the patient enters the operating room, the healing journey has already begun. Dr. Rob uses a range of cutting-edge tools and techniques to put the body and mind into a deeply relaxed, parasympathetic state—the optimal physiological environment for rapid, efficient recovery.

And the support doesn't stop there. In the critical first week following the procedure, patients visit Dr. Rob's clinic to undergo targeted lymphatic drainage and hyperbaric oxygen therapy, which have been shown to accelerate the healing process dramatically.

The real magic happens in the months that follow as patients continue to implement the comprehensive SHARP protocol. With the guidance of Dr. Rob's expert team, they transition from the clinical environment back into their daily lives, armed with the knowledge, skills, and support systems they need to maintain their momentum.

It's a level of holistic, patient-centered care that I've rarely seen in the medical world. As someone who has undergone my fair share of medical procedures, I can attest to the profound difference it can make.

My journey into the world of surgical healing programs began with my work on ABC's *Extreme Makeover* show, where I had to convince the medical staff of the benefits of proper recovery tools. The resistance I faced was reminiscent of the times I had to sneak supplements and other healing modalities into the hospital to support my son's recovery in the ICU.

When my son was in the ICU following a serious accident, I took it upon myself to create a comprehensive healing regimen, incorporating everything from targeted nutrition and specialized supplements to soothing music and aromatherapy. The results were nothing short of miraculous, defying the grim prognosis that the doctors had initially given. It was clear to me then, as it is now, that the importance of post-surgical care was vastly underestimated.

That's why I'm so passionate about Dr. Rob's work. He is single-handedly redefining the standard of care for surgical patients, ushering in a new era of holistic, integrative medicine. By treating the whole person, not just the surgical site, he is helping his patients achieve outcomes that were once unimaginable.

I've seen it firsthand in my own life and repeatedly in the lives of Dr. Rob's patients. No matter the procedure, the results are consistently exceptional. Patients emerge from their surgeries not just physically transformed but also mentally, emotionally, and spiritually renewed.

The key lies in Dr. Rob's unwavering commitment to the recovery process. He understands that surgery is only one piece of the puzzle—a critical piece, to be sure, but one that must be nested within a comprehensive, integrative framework to achieve the best possible outcomes.

That's why SHARP is so revolutionary. It looks at the patient's well-being as the North Star, guiding every decision and intervention. From the moment they walk through the door, patients are empowered to take an active role in their healing journey, collaborating with Dr. Rob's team to optimize their body, mind, and spirit for the challenges ahead.

With SHARP, patients have access to a vast arsenal of cutting-edge tools and techniques, all designed to accelerate healing, minimize discomfort, and restore them to a state of vibrant health.

It's a true paradigm shift in the world of surgical care, one that will become the new standard in the years to come. Dr. Rob's contributions to the field of surgery and recovery are a clarion call to patients, surgeons, and the medical community at large to adopt a more holistic, patient-centered approach.

As we turn the pages of this book, let Dr. Rob's vision and dedication inspire us. Let us see surgery not as an isolated event but as a journey that, with the right preparation and care, can lead to successful outcomes and a transformation that encompasses the whole person. In this comprehensive approach to surgery and recovery, Dr. Rob offers us a glimpse into the future of medical care, where every patient's journey to health is supported, nurtured, and valued.

JJ Virgin

Celebrity Nutrition and Fitness Expert

# Free 20 Minute Training

**DO YOU SUFFER FROM BREAST IMPLANT ILLNESS?**

Watch this Free 20 minute Fast Class

## The SHARP™ Method:

**The 5 must do's to accelerate healing and recovery time pre and post surgery.**

Over 9000 surgeries later, Dr Rob Whitfield, MD reveals his secrets for successful treatment of BII and preparing women for Explant Surgery.

WATCH THE FAST CLASS NOW

**IN THIS FAST CLASS YOU WILL DISCOVER:**

- Increased understanding on how your unique body can accelerate and optimize healing
- Identify all the markers that can lead to the symptoms requiring correction
- Turn any surgery into a premium revitalization experience
- Teach you how to capture energy and preserve your youth
- Rebalance your entire body for the new YOU
- A holistic approach to preparing the body for surgery

SIGN UP BELOW TO ACCESS Dr. ROB'S FAST CLASS:

WATCH NOW

# INTRODUCTION

It's never easy to decide to pay for surgical treatment, even if it will help you live your best life. The period leading up to treatment can be a time of great doubt and anxiety. But if you've opened this book, congratulations. The worst part is already behind you. Not only have you decided to go ahead with treatment, but by picking up my book, you've also decided to take control of your recovery.

You're holding everything you need to do that in your hands.

People get nervous about treatment for many reasons, and I'll explain later why you don't need to worry about any of them. But one of the most common reasons people get anxious is the thought of a long period of recovery after any treatment. They imagine they'll be stuck at home, missing out on being active, catching up with friends, and attending social occasions.

The surgical recovery program I will describe means that those days are past. I'll tell you everything you need to know about preparing for treatment in a way that leverages the power of your body's systems to recover as quickly as possible.

I call it SHARP: the Strategic Holistic Accelerated Recovery Program. It's strategic because it lays out a unique pathway for each patient suited to their needs. It means a planned recovery rather than constantly changing to react to circumstances. It's holistic because it treats the whole body, not just the site of the procedure, and it makes the procedure part of a far larger journey from preparation to recovery. Using your genetic profile, exposure to toxins, hormones, nutrition, and gut health, the program leverages your body's natural healing powers. The program is accelerated because it simply speeds up the process of recovery.

With SHARP, your recovery has begun before you even enter the operating room. That way, you can return quicker to feeling great and living your daily life.

It might be that no one will even notice you've been away.

## Power of Recovery

Everyone who comes to see me in my clinic in Austin, Texas, wants the same things: treatment that will help them feel better about themselves physically, mentally, and emotionally and a full and quick recovery. They trust me to provide the treatment, and my team and I show them how they can help themselves with the second part, the recovery.

The holy grail is a successful treatment followed by a rapid recovery. And the good news is that thousands of women have already achieved it.

I've been a plastic surgeon for over 20 years, starting from my training in microsurgery and oncologic surgery, when I reconstructed tissue destroyed by cancer or skin destroyed by burns. That's when I first became interested in the recovery process.

Many traditional surgeons' interest ends once the treatment is done. Their training and skill lie in their abilities in the operating room, so they leave the recovery process in the hands of the nurses and the patients themselves. It's not like that when you're reconstructing skin for burn victims. In that situation, the speed of recovery can make the difference between life and death.

When I worked with burn victims, I became fascinated by the different speeds at which people recovered from treatment and what might be slowing down recovery for those who did not respond so well.

Many of the answers lay in how people lived before the treatment. Some of the reasons were obvious: they ate junk food, they drank too much alcohol, they didn't get enough sleep, and they were constantly stressed.

That meant it must be possible to improve the prospects for a quick recovery by making sensible changes before or after the treatment. We could help people improve their diet, drinking, and sleeping patterns. We could help them live in a quieter, more sanitary environment.

The fact remained that some patients still recovered more slowly than others. Medical practitioners didn't know precisely why back then, although we suspected it might be related to their genes. Now we understand that we were right.

Recovery starts at a genetic level.

The word "genetic" might bother you. We all know that in some circles, genetics get a bad rap. The media is full of stories about people "misusing" or "abusing" genetics. As an experienced clinician, I can tell you those stories are all garbage. Genetics is nothing more than understanding how your body works based on some of the most exciting scientific developments of the last two decades.

Genetics is the study of genes, and your genes are a unique pattern of chemical messengers that control every cell in your body. You inherit your genes from your parents. Our genes decide if we'll be tall or short, fair or dark, healthy or prone to disease. On another level, they control how all 30 trillion individual cells of our body behave: how our cells reproduce, use energy, or react to being sick or having treatment. Our growing understanding of genetics has become the foundation for substantial medical advances in recent decades.

That's why I will discuss genetics far more in this book than you would probably expect from a plastic surgeon. I know your genetic makeup is fundamental to guaranteeing the best recovery possible from treatment.

With the proper training, a physician who knows your genetic makeup can use that knowledge to get your body into the most effective state for recovering from treatment effects. The secret is combining traditional medicine and cutting-edge science to prime your body's ability to heal and restore you to total health quickly.

## Maximize Your Recovery

When we were younger, our elders told us to get a good night's sleep, not to eat between meals, and to eat plenty of fruit and vegetables. People have always known that this kind of stuff helps us stay healthy. It's not rocket science. Our parents teach us to do things that will improve our overall health.

(By health, by the way, I'm not just referring to our physical condition. It's also our physical, mental, emotional, or spiritual well-being. Cosmetic treatment is physical, but it has a substantial emotional component, with many patients having underlying issues such as guilt. That's why, in my practice, I have multiple patient concierges who support our patients. Their support can be as crucial for a full recovery as the physical protocols.)

It's evident that we can recover quicker after treatment by being as healthy as possible *before* treatment. Good overall health matters for recovery because the immune system, which helps the body recover from disease or injury, is finely tuned. It's fragile. Many aspects of our daily lives can tip it out of balance, from what we eat to how we sleep. That's why we read so much in the press or hear so much in the media about autoimmune diseases and other problems caused by people's immune function working poorly.

If your immune system is out of balance, it won't be as effective, so you'll recover from illness or treatment more slowly.

Let's explore the immune system for a moment to understand its role. It's a system of defenses against illness and injury. When our immune system detects anything harmful within the body, such as an infection or a wound, it sends special cells to the site to destroy dangerous germs or to repair damaged cells. As they do their work, those special cells cause inflammation or swelling.

There are two types of inflammation: acute and chronic.

We're all familiar with acute inflammation. If someone trips in a hole and twists their ankle, the joint swells and becomes painful. It might feel hot to the touch and be very red. That's acute inflammation. It might last a few hours or a few days, but once the special cells have repaired the internal effects of the injury, the body turns off the immune system. The swelling and pain disappear.

Chronic inflammation lasts longer than acute inflammation and has a less immediate cause. It's also less visible than acute inflammation but potentially more harmful. It takes place within the body. We're generally not aware of it. It can affect vital organs, such as the brain, heart, lungs, and liver, or body parts, such as the joints, muscles, blood vessels, or nerves.

In chronic inflammation, the cells that stimulate inflammation just keep working. The immune system doesn't switch itself off, leading to diseases such as Hashimoto's, which mainly affects women. In Hashimoto's, the immune system attacks cells in the thyroid.

The thyroid is a small gland in the front of the neck that controls our hormones, stimulating the body's cells and tissues. Thyroid-related conditions lead to tiredness, weight gain, and loss of muscle strength, so Hashimoto's can be a severe condition.

Before any treatment, it's critical to restore the immune system to balance so it can help with recovery. To do that, we need to reduce chronic inflammation. The best way to do that is by understanding why the immune system is overstimulated in the first place and then figuring out how to lower the stimulation.

Chronic inflammation is usually the result of two things: the environment you live in and your genetic makeup.

Our environment includes anything from the food we eat and drink to the air we breathe, the house we live in, and even the soap we use. Which specific environmental elements trigger reactions in our bodies is decided by our genetic makeup. Some things trigger chronic inflammation in virtually everyone, and others only trigger particular people. But for almost everyone, environmental elements cause chronic inflammation and never stop causing it.

## You and Your Genes

We ingest things into our bodies daily that can cause chronic inflammation. These harmful substances range from artificial preservatives in processed food to pollutants in water and smoke particles in the air.

In the past, doctors suspected that the ability of each individual's body to deal with individual substances or harmful toxins was conditioned by their genes. Now, we know how that happens. Specific combinations of genes can increase or decrease your ability to process particular substances to avoid inflammation.

That's why the first step of my surgical recovery program is to understand your genetic profile. Some people think it's odd that a plastic surgeon would be so interested in genes, but genetics are the best way for me to tailor my surgical recovery program to individuals.

I get all my patients to take a simple genetic test. Don't worry: this isn't Frankenstein stuff. It's basic science. All you have to do is provide a saliva sample that gets sent to a recommended laboratory for analysis. I've researched the process by having my genetic analysis done by various laboratories, so I only recommend the most reliable and valuable tests I know.

Once we understand your genetic profile, I can help boost your immune system by using carefully created supplements to achieve optimal recovery. My clinicians have developed a range of supplements to help support most genetic limitations that impede the body's normal functioning.

Meanwhile, anyone preparing for treatment can benefit from improving a few essential lifestyle elements, regardless of their genetic profile. I always tell people, "You can't pick your parents, and you can't outrun a bad diet." By that, I mean that you can't change the genes you're born with, but you *can* improve many things that will increase your body's ability to recover sufficiently, such as eating better food, drinking purer water, and breathing cleaner air.

As we'll see, if you start doing any of those things today, you can improve your immune system's ability to recover and overall health.

We can see this improvement by measuring heart-rate variability, or HRV, which records how much your heart rate changes in different situations. It's a key indicator of your physiological health that many wearable monitors on watches or wristbands now measure. A high HRV shows that your body and immune system can handle change and stress well. A low HRV shows that you're less able physiologically to react to changing circumstances.

If you make small changes in what you eat, drink, and breathe or how you sleep, your HRV will rise. The improvements will be exponential if you compound those changes by understanding your genetics, improving your body's ability to eliminate toxins, and ensuring that your vitamins and hormones are balanced.

## Part I: Preparation

This book is divided into three sections: Preparation, Treatment, and Post-Operative.

The first part, Preparation, is the longest because the foundations for recovery are laid before the treatment even begins. I'll show you how to prepare for treatment by understanding and improving five main areas of your health: genetics, toxins, nutrition, hormones, and your gut microbiome. Most clinicians know that each of these areas impacts the body's ability to recover, but few connect the dots the way I have to see how they all fit together.

### Genetics

- Your genes are the foundation of your recovery program.
- Full recovery is linked to the effectiveness of four "pathways" controlled by your genes by which the body absorbs vital vitamins and other substances that maintain the immune system. If those pathways are not working well, they slow down recovery.
- I have developed a range of supplements to boost your genetic profile and make those pathways as efficient as possible.

## Toxicity

- The environment is full of toxic substances, such as black mold, smoke from fires, auto exhausts, or industry. You breathe in these particles or spores without even realizing it, and they cause inflammation in your lungs and other problems.
- Parabens, used as artificial preservatives in cosmetics, and phthalates, used to make plastics, soaps, and hairsprays, disrupt the endocrine system. This leads to an imbalance of the female hormones estrogen, progesterone, and testosterone, which affects women's metabolism, mood, sleep, and other behaviors.
- Preparation before treatment involves eliminating environmental toxins and using supplements to help the body detoxify.

## Nutrition

When it comes to food, everyone already knows the basic rules.

- Cut out processed foods, which are full of artificial preservatives and colorants.
- Avoid bad fats and bad carbs, gluten, and dairy.
- Eat more protein and healthier fats from avocados, seeds, and oily fish.
- Don't eat white bread, cake, or cookies.
- Get your sugar from fruit, not from candy or soda.
- Drink filtered water.
- If you drink alcohol, limit it to the weekends.
- Drink organic wine or spirits (low in sulfur) rather than beer, which contains gluten, which causes inflammation.

- Hacking your diet is easy, and even minor adjustments will contribute to faster recovery.

## Gut Microbiome

- Your gut is home to 100 trillion microscopic cells that help digest food, clear out the body's waste, and regulate the immune system.
- If the gut microbiome becomes unbalanced, it works less efficiently.
- An unbalanced microbiome lowers the gut's ability to absorb food nutrients, preventing the body from getting the nutrients and vitamins it needs. It also reduces the body's ability to eliminate waste, so toxins build up inside.
- The gut-brain axis means the brain doesn't receive as much energy as it needs and becomes less effective.

## Hormones

- Hormones are chemical messengers within the body. The body produces hormones to stimulate cells to control functions from digestion and sleep patterns to mood. Hormones are made by the endocrine system, which includes several different glands.
- The thyroid produces hormones that help regulate our metabolism. If the thyroid is not working correctly, losing weight or sculpting your body shape is difficult.
- Endocrine dysfunction can cause particular problems for women. They may become hypothyroid when they have such high inflammation that their thyroid doesn't function well. They may always be stressed out because they have too much estrogen, cortisol, and low thyroid function. High levels of estrogen and its metabolites

can cause anxiety, bad cycle pain, and cramps, as well as contribute to conditions such as endometriosis and polycystic ovarian syndrome.

- The surgical recovery program recommends specific supplements to boost your genetic profile and restore the endocrine system to a healthy balance.

## Part II: Treatment

The book's second part describes what happens when patients come to the clinic in Austin for treatment.

By this time, they've used a combination of changes to their diet, environmental improvements, and specific supplements to prepare their bodies as well as possible for recovery. We also get them in the right mindset so they're not stressed or anxious.

The treatment itself is straightforward. I don't use surgical drains because we have learned that they are not necessary. The most efficient fluid removal system is the body's own lymphatic system. Without drains there is far less discomfort and almost no chance of infection. Our anesthesia providers are always optimizing the experience by avoiding the use of narcotics.

## Part III: After the Treatment

The last part of the book describes the recovery process, from the day after the operation to the final medical sign-off a year later.

- From the day after treatment, patients have the advantage of special therapies at my clinical center to encourage their body's healing.
- Once they leave the clinic, patients now understand how important it is to continue to recover in a quiet,

pleasant atmosphere, with great food, high air quality, and temperature control so they can reduce the temperature at night to help them sleep better.

- They continue to use our supplementation program to keep their body systems working at their most efficient.

This part of the book will show you how to act consciously to ensure your health is as good as possible, which is how you'll recover quickly.

## New Understanding of Recovery

There are many books about surgical recovery. Virtually all of them are out of date. They're all based on an assumption that recovery happens at its speed. They don't reflect how understanding genetics can speed up the process.

People who rest and stay free of infection usually recover well from treatment. What many surgeons and other practitioners don't realize, though, is that recovery is not passive. It's something patients can take charge of themselves to achieve their own best results.

The surgical recovery program I describe in this book gives you that power.

Over thousands of cases where I've treated people with cancers, burns, and other injuries, I've worked with leading practitioners and mentors to investigate how to improve recovery outcomes. As I studied more and more approaches, I developed a program to help patients get back to their daily lives quicker after treatment.

I figured out my surgical recovery program over a 25-year career in the public and private health systems in the United States and Europe that few surgeons can match. My natural curiosity means I constantly keep up with the latest technology and techniques that can improve surgical outcomes—for me and my patients.

I want to help you understand your body so you're empowered to make decisions about your health. Think of this book as pulling the drapes back to show you how your body works. If you don't understand that, you cannot make choices.

I developed my expertise to ensure the best recovery outcomes for my patients. I'm not sharing it just to be altruistic. I'm sharing it because it makes my job easier if I show you how to do this yourself without waiting for me to tell you what you need to do.

The idea of treatment is always scary, especially if it's a treatment you've chosen to have. Many people don't go through with it. But suppose you're investing your dollars, euros, or pounds in getting this right. In that case, you want the best possible outcome to optimize your investment: not just your financial investment but your emotional and physical investment.

If you know you need a different type of treatment, say because your joints are wearing, you might be putting it off because of fear. In that case, I hope this book can help you decide to move forward. I know how easy it is to delay treatment. I've had five knee surgeries, and I need a knee replacement that I keep putting off.

Most of my techniques aren't unique, and some are very familiar. You might recognize elements of different medical traditions such as integrative medicine, allopathic medicine, functional medicine, and natural medicine. One of my fundamental beliefs is that I don't care what anything is called as long as it fulfills one criterion: it has to provide the best outcome for the patient.

By combining ideas that have been around forever—like eating well or getting enough sleep—with functional genetics that we didn't even know about a decade ago, the program maximizes everyone's prospects of a quick recovery.

## Who Am I?

Let me tell you a bit more about myself. People don't necessarily know how to take me. I don't look much like their idea of a surgeon because I don't wear suits, I usually wear sandals, and my hair is either very short or long, like a courtier from 17th-century France. I look tired virtually all the time. And you know what? I don't care.

At this point in my life, I'm not here to make an impression on anybody. I'm here because I understand the issues that make people like you decide to have paid-for treatment. Other clinics see three people like you in a month; I see 40 people like you in a week. I've done thousands of treatments like these from many years ago until today.

I'm not a genius. I've just been curious enough to ask the questions and not be satisfied with the answers. If you remain curious, you should never simply accept the status quo.

Some of what I'll tell you is still unusual in plastic surgery, like my focus on genetics. But it's all based on mountains of data. When you have a reputation as a disruptor like mine, you must ensure that everything you say can be backed up. Nothing in the program isn't backed up by overwhelming scientific evidence.

I'd been a surgeon for nearly 20 years before I started my solo private practice. I specialize in breast explant operations and provide a full range of advanced cosmetic treatments, including my patented No-Cut Facelift. Having my private practice made sense because my enthusiasm for trying new techniques had always gotten me in trouble, with other doctors telling me, "You can't say that." Now, no one gets to say that anymore.

That's how I was able to bring breast implant illness to national awareness after users on social media began to identify its symptoms.

Most doctors ignored it, making me even more determined to raise its profile. I understand the immense emotions involved in deciding to have implants and also to have them removed. I also know how difficult it can be for women to finally figure out that an implant is causing them a problem, by which time they are often sick.

I believe that I'm an outlier in a whole movement that will shift the focus on plastic surgery from treatment alone to improving patients' recovery. I'm already spreading the surgical recovery program to surgical practices nationwide. Those practices will do a better job with their patients. Their patient engagement will be better, their understanding of problems will be more significant, and the program will spread as practitioners begin to understand that this program will get far better results than whatever they are doing currently.

At the moment, some of my medical colleagues would know very little about what I'm telling you. It's fair to say that some of them would probably scoff a little that a plastic surgeon should be so interested in something as "advanced" as genetics.

People like that are on the wrong side of history.

Medicine is changing quicker now than it ever has. We still know comparatively little about functional genomics and biophysics or the role of genetics and physics in how our cells work, but what we know already shows us that these will play a huge role in medicine. Genetic analysis, sound therapy, light therapy, electromagnetic field therapy: new developments are happening in many fields that will change the face of treatment and patient care.

These new technologies will be like a rocket ship to a new level of medicine. At the moment, we're still taking the stairs with a broken leg and a cane. We're not getting anywhere fast.

Some doctors haven't yet realized how influential these new therapies will be. They didn't learn about them in training, so they find it difficult to take them seriously. Some cutting-edge therapies are still waiting for official approval because the approval process is slow and bureaucratic. I don't think it ever helps people to close their minds to change. Medical practitioners should be prepared to use whatever advances benefit their patients, as long as they are safe and efficient, from understanding any issues you might have in detoxifying to getting into the proper mindset and ready for treatment.

If you're a patient, your results will improve, your recovery will be quicker, and your satisfaction rate can increase.

The surgical recovery program improves quality. As science and the available technology improve, the program will also change, as we'll see in the book's last chapter.

The key to the whole program is to make your recovery proactive rather than reactive. The program prepares you for treatment rather than simply dealing with the treatment's results.

The sooner you start, the better your outcome will be.

So let's get started.

PART I

# PREPARATION

CHAPTER 1

# Immunity and Inflammation

Do you know someone who never gets sick? Their body seems indestructible. They're out and about in flu season and don't get a sniffle; they always work out and never get sore muscles; they breathe in fire smoke and it doesn't bother them.

What makes those people unique is their immune system, which is the defense that protects the body from disease and heals us when we get sick or suffer an injury. Those people's immune systems are in near-perfect balance, meaning they have higher resistance to infection and faster recovery rates than most of us.

If you were in charge of the government, you'd want those people in your special forces. Virtually nothing can stop them.

Your immune system protects you from germs that cause disease and other substances that can harm the body in the short or long term, such as toxins. We get exposed to harmful substances or toxins in the air we breathe and what we eat and drink. Our skin is a barrier against them, as are defenses in our noses, mouths, and throats, but toxins can still enter the body through the skin or through normal breathing, eating, and drinking.

If your body can't protect itself, these germs and toxins will make you ill. Your immune system is your body's police force. It's there to defend you. Your body recognizes certain substances or cell structures that are put into it and doesn't react to them. Those substances are free to enter. If your body doesn't recognize substances, on the other hand, it assumes that they're harmful, and the immune system tries to put up a barrier or to get rid of them. The weaker your immune system, however, the more it struggles to deal with whatever the body doesn't recognize, and the higher your exposure risk.

A weak immune system exposes you to more stress. You'll get more colds. You may have gut trouble. It may take a long time to heal if you get a cut. You may feel permanently tired. All those are potential signs of a problem with your immune system.

## Inflammation

One of the most powerful tools of our immune system is inflammation. It's the injury response.

Inflammation occurs when white blood cells release chemicals to attack microbes, germs, or foreign objects that enter the body or to heal damage if you've suffered an injury. On the outside of the body, inflammation can cause pain, heat, redness, or swelling, such as the swelling that occurs if you fall and sprain your ankle. Inside the body, inflammation causes swelling around our organs and blood vessels.

As we've seen, when a sprained ankle causes acute inflammation, the immune system is activated. The white blood cells do their thing, the injury heals, and the signal for inflammation is turned off.

In chronic inflammation, the signal never gets turned off. That can lead to harmful symptoms in all the body's major systems: neurologic, cardiac, pulmonary, musculoskeletal, and digestive.

Chronic inflammation damages the organs. It drains energy from our cells, making the body systems less effective. It produces fluid, which causes swelling. Anything that causes swelling around any vital structure, whether a nerve, organ, or brain, is always bad.

High levels of inflammation make it difficult for people to lose weight. Overweight people usually carry more inflammation than slim people because fat stores a lot of toxins. Overweight people get blood-sugar problems or other metabolic issues from what they eat. If you feel puffy, that's a result of inflammation.

You can initially reduce chronic inflammation by cutting out a few types of food from your diet: gluten, dairy, beer, and wine. If you do the surgical recovery program, you can lose 10 pounds simply by losing the fluid accumulated from inflammation in your gastrointestinal (GI) tract or extremities.

As we'll see in Chapter 4, the surgical recovery program recommends a diet similar to a keto diet: one that's high in good fats and protein and low in carbohydrates and gluten. That diet alone will reduce inflammation, but once you've adapted to it, you can also try to figure out what specific foods might trigger inflammation for you.

When you have too much inflammation, none of the checks and balances that keep your body healthy work. The immune system is running flat out but not getting anywhere. That means it has less energy to help you recover from treatment. Inflammation also affects the thyroid function and sex hormones that drive your metabolism. Because your metabolism increases your capacity to heal, a poorly functioning metabolism limits your ability to recover.

Inflammation in your blood vessels can damage the organs, such as the skin, the liver, or the kidneys. Inflammation blocks the vessels, leading to high or low blood pressure. Both too-high and too-low blood pressure damage the kidneys. Inflammation plus too much alcohol causes cirrhosis in the liver. You can't detoxify, so you become yellow because your liver can't get toxic ammonia out of your body, which can be fatal. If your brain has too high a blood pressure, you might have a stroke. If not enough oxygen reaches the heart, you might have a heart attack.

Ultimately, inflammation in the muscles or blood vessels is a major underlying cause of death.

Neural inflammation—inflammation of the nerves—is a slightly special case. It causes memory loss, brain fog, and light and sound sensitivity. It often occurs in people who suffer from mold exposure, which is present in many homes and the wine we like to drink.

When people complain of headaches or memory loss but their MRI doesn't show any problems, they can often have chronic neural inflammation. The inflammation affects the central nervous system (CNS), which comprises the brain and spinal cord. The CNS controls how we move, think, feel, and learn. Inflammation can also move to the peripheral nervous system, the nerves that connect the CNS to the body's organs and limbs. If the peripheral nervous system is inflamed, people will feel burning in their extremities, experience nerve pain down their legs, or experience a tremor throughout their whole body.

Neural inflammation is usually chronic rather than acute, but anything that affects your central or peripheral nervous system can cause intense pain.

Neural inflammation is usually the result of environmental toxins. That's one of the reasons I have my patients do a toxicity profile test so we understand how they live. If they live in a home with mold and eat poor-quality food and drink low-quality water, they're not going to recover as we would want them to—and as they would like to.

## Reducing Inflammation

When patients arrive at my clinic for treatment, I like them to have as little internal inflammation as possible. There are a couple of important reasons. First, the therapy will cause new inflammation, and I want to avoid overwhelming the immune system. Second, any inflammation that already exists impairs immune function, so it will reduce the efficiency of the body's healing process and slow down recovery.

Anyone preparing for surgical treatment should lower their baseline inflammation as much as possible. That means looking at the causes of their chronic inflammation. In chronic inflammation, as we've seen, the immune system stays on because you're doing something that keeps it turned on. If you eat poorly, it stays on. If you ingest fluids contaminated with arsenic, it stays on. It stays on if you breathe air with mold in it or use products that contain parabens. Those things stimulate your immune system without knowing it, causing chronic inflammation.

In the following chapters, I'll explain how you can reduce inflammation before treatment by following simple steps and supplementing, such as taking a couple of grams of Omega 3 daily. Losing weight will also help.

Most of these steps involve learning how to live as the best possible version of yourself. This is a playbook for becoming the best you. Even if you don't have an upcoming surgery, if you ran this playbook for its own sake, you would experience life better.

At the core of reducing inflammation is your metabolism, the chemical processes within the body that keep you alive, and how you detoxify. Hormones control the metabolism.

Inflammation affects all hormones, starting with the thyroid and then sex hormones. In women, inflammation often affects the sex hormone estrogen (men don't have as much estrogen as women). If a woman converts most of her estrogen to toxic estrogen, she'll be at risk for anxiety, bad periods, heavy bleeding, endometriosis, and polycystic ovarian syndrome.

As we'll see in the next chapter, if you don't detoxify well in the key pathways by which the body absorbs critical vitamins and minerals, and if you have impaired estrogen metabolism, you become estrogen dominant. Together with high levels of cortisol and poor detoxification, this puts you in a constant state of fight or flight, which is highly stressful because your body is primed to react as if it is facing an external threat. You're anxious, and you don't sleep well. You're fatigued and may have gut trouble, liver dysfunction, or even brittle bones. With low testosterone, you have poor focus, limited hair and nail growth, and less energy. You don't feel like working out—and you certainly have no libido.

Overall, women with poor estrogen metabolism probably don't feel too good.

We use supplements to restore proper hormone function. People's thyroids start working better, so the hormones are absorbed better. There's more about this in Chapter 6.

One of my patients was a woman in her twenties who had gained 60 pounds in a decade after she got implants when she was 17. She was on so many medicines she was a zombie.

She was a victim of a cycle that usually goes like this. The primary doctor puts you on antidepressants, and then they put you on something to help you sleep, and then they put you on something to give you energy. So you take pills to wake up and stay awake, and you take more pills to go to sleep. Then, you take more pills to prevent you from feeling depressed about taking so many medications.

Meanwhile, if you eat and detoxify badly, you don't sleep well, and because you only recover when you're asleep, your body never truly recovers.

That cycle just rinses and repeats.

That's why we have to use genetics to fix your inflammation.

CHAPTER 2

# Genetics

Those special forces folks we met in the last chapter who don't have any chronic inflammation got lucky. They have an optimal function in the pathways by which they process Vitamin D, Vitamin C, and other chemicals essential for metabolism and the immune system. That comes down to their genes.

When people say, "It's all in the genes," they're right. Virtually everything about us comes down to our genes. Our genes are like instructions that control how our cells work. In turn, our cells control how our bodies react to food and drink, how we sleep, how we get rid of toxins and other waste, how we generate essential nutrients and chemicals for the body's most important functions, and how we recover.

Genetics get a bad rap. It's a bit of a trigger word for alarmists who talk about genetics as if they were talking about some kind of sinister Frankenstein plot to change the nature of humans. That's just because most people don't understand what genetics is. They get all their information from inexpert journalists or social media. I don't want to go too deep into the science, but genetics is natural.

It's not something that's been invented by a crazy scientist. It's always going on in every living thing on the planet. Nothing is alarming about it at all. It's simply a process that will show us more about how our bodies work if we can understand it better.

Genes are a series of chemical signals we inherit from our parents that instruct the cells of our body how to behave. If our bodies are factories for turning food, water, and oxygen into energy and eliminating the waste they produce, our genes are the managers telling each department how to work. But our genes aren't always perfect. They change or mutate in tiny ways that sometimes have a significant impact. In some cases, they can cause different physical or mental impairments in babies. More commonly, they impact tiny parts of an individual's life. Genes are complicated sequences of chemicals that are different in everyone, even within the same family. They're why one sibling is allergic to seafood, but another isn't; you might have astigmatism, but your partner has perfect vision, or you can shake off a cold quickly when your friend gets a cold that lingers for weeks.

Researchers have mapped the whole human genome in the past two decades, the complete sequence of billions of genetic variations that make us human. This monumental breakthrough has given scientists a much deeper understanding of our genes' role in all our lives. That understanding is already leading to considerable advances in the kind of medicine that I've followed throughout my career.

Those advances underlie the most up-to-date versions of the surgical recovery program.

Early in my career, I realized people recovered from treatments and injuries at different speeds. Now, we can even identify the specific individual genes or combinations of genes responsible for such variations. Genetics make it much easier to understand why people get anxious, for example, or why they might feel under the weather when there's nothing wrong with them.

It's not as simple as saying, "This gene causes this result," however. Your genetics set the baseline for how you react to particular substances, but they are also conditioned by your environment and how you eat, drink, and sleep. One time, for example, I was living with my family in a rental … and felt terrible all the time. So, I had a toxicology report done (they usually just involve supplying a urine sample). The report showed that my body was full of toxins that limited my cellular function: mold from the house, but also bisphenol, butyl parabens, glyphosates, and propyl parabens.

It's a toxic brew.

Where did they come from? In Texas, everyone is constantly exposed to mold in the air and their homes. (We now know, by the way, that exposure to mold causes neural inflammation, which can increase anxiety.) Bisphenol can come from drinking out of plastic bottles or heating food in plastic containers, which you should never do. Glyphosate is a herbicide and crop desiccant used to kill weeds that often get into foods. Butyl parabens come from haircare products and male shaving creams. Propyl parabens come from shaving cream, lotion, or shampoo.

We must do what we can to limit our exposure to substances that might harm our bodies, including the environment, what we eat and drink, and the air we breathe. If you have the chance to breathe filtered air, take it! We should also limit our risk by using fewer plastics, buying food not farmed with artificial chemicals, and washing fresh produce.

We should also change or supplement our genes to get our bodies in optimum condition for recovery. However, before we see how that works, let's look a bit more at the role of genetics in our lives.

## The Role of Genes

Combinations of genes control every element of our interaction with the world: our pleasure response, our addictive behavior response, our mood, and whether we put on or lose weight quickly. Our genetic profile is coupled with how we sleep and breathe, what we eat and drink, where we live, and whether we have clean air in the mountains or coming off the ocean.

Let's look at four areas where genetics affects how your body reacts to the environment.

- **Exercise:** Most people get sore after strenuous exercise, perhaps for a few days. They usually assume it's because of lactic acid buildup, but that's only partly true. It's also because the activity level of their body's enzymes—the proteins that speed up our bodies' chemical processes—is limited by the genetics they inherited from their parents.

  I advise my patients against exercising on a peloton, spin, or high-intensity cardio, all of which build up lactic acid. I recommend walking outdoors, especially up hills, and lifting weights.

  The weights don't have to be heavy. As we get above 35, we all start to lose muscle mass thanks to sarcopenia. The best way to avoid this is by lifting weights to preserve our muscle tone. Don't worry. This isn't about being like bodybuilders in the gym. Think of it as being more like farmers who lift and carry things all the time in their daily lives, so they're strong without bulking up.

- **Sleep:** Some people don't sleep properly because of the genes that regulate their circadian rhythm. If we can identify the genes involved, we can develop supplements to help those people sleep better. (Of course, anyone can also take simple, practical steps to augment their sleep. Sit away from the TV screen. Don't use phones or tablets at night; switch all electronics off an hour before bed. Make sure the temperature of the room you sleep in is cool.)

The minimum amount of sleep we need every night is about six and a half hours, though eight hours is better. We lose cognitive ability if we sleep for less than six hours. The military has conducted research that found that soldiers' ability to execute a task well goes down if they get less sleep than that.

No one would ever want to be on patrol with a soldier who hadn't gotten their sleep.

Sleep is also vital because it's only while we're asleep that our bodies secrete growth hormone, which helps us recover from injury and repair muscle tissue after exercise. That's why it's essential to have about two hours of deep sleep every night to recover, supported by the appropriate electrolytes and protein levels in your diet.

I encourage people to use biometric devices to monitor their sleep, such as sleep mats or wearables.

- **Diet:** Genes play a crucial role in every aspect of our diet, including why some people binge on food at night. Some people don't absorb nutrition well, so they feel hungry even after eating or don't consume enough protein, which has the same effect. People might eat a lot of food without it being taken into their bodies because it's a type of food their gut can't absorb or because it's not high enough in nutrients. It just passes through them as if they never ate anything—and they keep eating.
- **Behavior:** A bad temper, a tendency to cry in movies, and even FOMO are all controlled by our genes, as is most of our behavior. Addictive behavior, for example, is a genetic predisposition shaped by a function of three genes. How your body manages those genes and your exposures can be the difference between someone who has OCD to the

point of finding it difficult to function and someone who is driven in business or life.

I ask all my patients to do a genetics test. I've already said I've had a number myself, so I know the labs I recommend are reliable. (I never recommend a therapy unless I've tried it myself first if possible.) I've started working with NVISN (https://www.nvisnlabs.com), a laboratory that uses genetics tests to test drug metabolism, so people can learn how their body copes with opioids or other medications. In general, genetics tests highlight areas where genetic issues might give rise to health problems and identify possible combinations of genes. My preferred test groups resulted in the following categories: Mood and Behavior, Immunity, Cardiovascular, Diet and Nutrition, Sleep and Hormones, Fitness, Body Type, and Drug Metabolism. The best tests also suggest ways to get around genetic problems, either by taking supplements or by altering our diet, lifestyle, and environment.

## Four Pathways

When it comes to the surgical recovery program specifically, our genes control four vital internal pathways I've already mentioned. These pathways convert vitamins into substances we need for our cells to function correctly. When our immune system and metabolism are less than optimal, it's often because of problems with one or more pathways. Any impairment of our metabolism will mean we find it more challenging to clear inflammation.

The pathways have complex-sounding names, but if I walk you through each one, you'll see that they're more straightforward than they sound.

### 1. Vitamin D Pathway

Lack of Vitamin D can cause particular problems in women who can't transport it, don't absorb it, or don't convert it into what their bodies need.

2. **Methylation Pathway**

   If you have problems with your methylation pathway, you can't process B vitamins (there are eight types). That can manifest as a cold that lasts forever, staying sore for days after a workout, or having nerve pain.

3. **Glutathione Pathway**

   Your glutathione pathway helps eliminate harmful environmental things you take into your body, such as mold, heavy metals, or products like washes and skincare. It prevents them from being absorbed and helps eliminate them.

4. **Antioxidant Pathway**

   As your cells create energy each day, they produce waste; if the waste isn't removed, it makes you feel fatigued. Clearing the trash is the task of antioxidants such as Vitamin C. They're like sanitation workers who take out the garbage.

The key to effective recovery is ensuring the proper B Vitamins, Vitamin D, Vitamin C, and magnesium before your treatment.

## Vitamin D Pathway

Vitamin D is essential for bone health, mood, and good cellular function, while a shortage can cause muscle cramps and a drop in calcium levels.

Vitamin D promotes calcium absorption in the gut, without which your muscles become weaker. If you don't absorb your food, a lack of calcium prevents your bones from mineralizing. The ultimate result can be osteoporosis, which is a particular problem for women—more than for men.

If your vitamin D pathway isn't working, your muscles don't contract properly. You'll get cramps and spasms and become hypocalcemic, meaning your calcium blood level will drop. Muscle function will be impaired, and your bones will not become strong.

Active Vitamin D comes from sunlight, but a combination of three genes controls its metabolism in the body. If these genes are not functioning correctly, Vitamin D doesn't get to where it needs to be. That weakens the immune system and the gut-brain axis, constantly making people tired and lethargic.

The bad news is that nearly everyone has genetic Vitamin D metabolism issues.

You could take the fittest of our special forces, but they would soon become weaker if they couldn't absorb food properly in their gut. Eventually, they couldn't run 5 feet without getting a cramp or a spasm. No matter how much milk they drink, they don't get enough calcium to strengthen their bones. And all because their Vitamin D pathway is off.

Without going into too much detail, the best way to compensate for this is by using my oral spray supplement, which uses Vitamin D3 K2 to activate the Vitamin D and then get it to where it needs to be in the gut to enable calcium absorption.

## Methylation Pathway

The methylation pathway is how the body absorbs Vitamin B, which gives you energy and control and is important in cellular functions. The methylation process involves up to nine genes, including the memorably named Motherf****r gene.

There are various B vitamins, and the best dietary sources are fish, organic eggs, organic spinach, and fortified nutritional yeast. People on vegan diets are usually lacking in B vitamins, as are people who have had a gastric bypass procedure.

B vitamins, stored in the liver once they are methylated, are essential for ensuring every cell in the body functions properly. They're used in all the tissues of the body. They help convert your food into energy, so people with B vitamin deficiency are constantly tired. B vitamins also help you create new blood cells and maintain skin and brain cells.

If your B Vitamin methylation pathway is limited, aerobic exercise will cause lactic acid buildup in your muscles. You shouldn't do any cardio; you should lift weights and walk. That will build up less lactic acid, so you won't have as much difficulty clearing it.

People with impaired metabolism, especially methylation, have many problems with inflammation. If you're prone to vascular or muscular inflammation, prolonged periods of intensive physical activity must be managed carefully because your body cannot handle their effects. If you have other genes that promote inflammation of your blood vessels, you may be more prone to a heart attack or stroke.

The simple solution is my mouth spray, which provides ready-methylated B Vitamins.

## Glutathione Pathway

Glutathione is an antioxidant that cleans the liver by removing environmental toxins such as molds, heavy metals, the breakdown products of smoking, and other harmful substances. If you can't detoxify, the immune system gets overloaded, and you feel poorly.

Strong smells are associated with the glutathione pathway. Because you don't detoxify well, you become more sensitive to odors. So, if you enter a room of smoke, perfume, or chemical odors and find them nasty, that's a genetic response. That's not something many people are aware of.

We have three ways to get rid of toxins from our bodies: sweat, poop, and pee. The main organs involved are the liver, kidneys, and skin, but the liver does most of the work because that's where all the toxins you take in eventually end up. The liver is a workhorse with various functions, including producing bile to help digestion, activating enzymes, and storing vitamins and minerals. It's your biggest internal organ, but it sometimes gets sluggish, which limits its ability to help clear toxins out of your body.

The liver stores glutathione, which helps bind the toxins we ingest from the environment, the air, or food, thus boosting the immune system. Then, the waste is excreted into your gastrointestinal (GI) tract.

Glutathione is your body's way to get rid of junk; if it can't, you have a huge problem. You're on a short road to a lot of trouble.

## Antioxidant Pathway

The antioxidant pathway uses two specific enzymes to clear the trash your cells produce through their normal functioning and get it out of your body. A poor antioxidant pathway makes you super sluggish, with extreme fatigue.

The trash is excreted into your GI tract, from where you pass it out as part of your poop, which is why people who have trouble with constipation usually have this waste stuck inside their body. The nervous system that controls their gut becomes impaired, decreasing their ability to expel toxins, and their whole metabolism suffers. One thing leads to another. The trash is stuck in their system. They can't detoxify metabolically because their genetics are impaired. They can't eliminate waste in their poop because they're constipated. Maybe they have problems sweating, so they can't get rid of it that way. That only leaves your pee. (Some people have issues pooping or sweating, but everybody pees: if you didn't, you'd die.)

People burden this pathway by eating a lot of processed junk food. We'll discuss food in Chapter 4, but if you're interested in the harm processed food does to our bodies, I recommend a book named *Metabolical* by Dr Robert Lustig. It will convince you to avoid processed foods and promote healthier options.

Ultra-processed foods include ice cream, ham, sausage, potato chips, mass-produced bread, breakfast cereals, biscuits, carbonated drinks, fruit-flavored yogurts, instant soups, and some forms of alcohol, including whiskey, gin, and rum. These are the worst examples. They contain way too much sugar and other chemicals.

If you're used to a diet of ultra-processed food and drink, I understand it's nearly impossible to change that behavior because it's established. Still, when preparing for treatment, you have a high degree of motivation to change. You've already committed to treatment, which comes with a significant investment in money, time, and emotion. If you can adapt your behavior for at least the weeks immediately before your treatment, you can help guarantee a better return on your investment by improving your ability for a quick recovery.

For example, I advise people not to drink beer and wine as they prepare for treatment, but I know I won't stop them from drinking alcohol altogether. That's too difficult a change to make. Instead, I have them drink a specific tequila that's ultra-filtered, so it contains far fewer chemicals than other liquor.

Regarding food, the best advice I can give is to shop on the periphery of the store, away from the big-selling, cheaply produced processed foods displayed in the middle. A helpful rule of thumb is that anything in a box doesn't come from the ground. Even with things you know came out of the ground, like fresh vegetables, you should check that they've been washed properly. In any case, wash them yourself at home. If you don't cleanse them, there's a good chance you'll eat insecticide or herbicide, which can harm the female endocrine system.

The efficiency of the antioxidant pathway can be increased by taking antioxidants such as Vitamin C, as well as mitochondrial supports, which include a variety of antioxidants, including vitamins, magnesium, manganese, creatinine, carnitine, and substances called adaptogens.

Most people are weakened in one or two of the four pathways. Someone weakened in three or four is in the worst of all situations. They don't detox well. Their body can't cope with the toxins they get from a bad diet, bad air, bad water, and the associated lack of sleep, day over day, month over month, year over year. When you can't detoxify your body, your immune system can't protect you from illnesses or harm. Your body's defenses are distracted. Your prospects for a good recovery are reduced.

CHAPTER 3

# Toxins

Some patients wonder why a plastic surgeon asks them to do a toxicology test. I'm sure some other plastic surgeons would wonder the same thing. It's because I know that treatment doesn't begin or end in the operating room and that detoxification is essential for the most effective recovery after treatment. A reliable tox test allows my team of detox practitioners to identify what we might be able to alter to enable a patient to improve their detoxification.

Ideally, patients who come for treatment would be completely free of toxins. In reality, that's almost impossible, so instead, we focus on getting out as many toxins as possible from their system. Toxicology slows recovery because it causes inflammation, reduces the body's efficiency, and limits the activation of the stem cells that the body uses for wound healing. Besides your genetics, nothing plays a more significant role in your recovery after a procedure than toxicology.

The more I know about someone, the better picture I have of how to maximize their recovery. That's why I look at their genetic analysis, their toxicity profile, their poop test, and their blood tests. Taken all together, they build a reliable portrait of a patient's physical condition.

When we try to understand what is happening inside someone's body, we don't know what we don't know. Even the best doctors miss 100 percent of things if they don't look for them, so I've always believed it's better to over-investigate. A toxicity profile might find things that a blood test will miss critical to understanding why someone behaves the way they do.

Take one of my patients, a 38-year-old firefighter. She was gaining weight and didn't understand why because she worked out regularly. She initially thought it might be menopause, but when we looked at her toxicity profile, it was clear that wasn't the cause of her issues.

She and her husband had mold in their home. She also grew up in a house where everybody smoked, so as a child, she was exposed to airborne acrylonitrile from cigarette smoke, which damages the lungs, liver, and central nervous system. That gave her massive exposure to a toxin called NACE, which comes from rubber and fibers that are included in tobacco and cigarettes. You don't need to have smoked yourself; if you grew up in a household where your parents smoked, you would have been exposed to it. If you also had genetic limitations on your pathways, you couldn't have cleared the NACE.

My patient also had two more toxins: glyphosate, which comes from chemicals used in food, and BPA, one of the highest-volume chemicals produced worldwide. BPA makes plastics for water bottles, sports equipment, CDs, and DVDs. Epoxy resin containing BPA is used to make water pipes, coat the inside of food and beverage cans, and make thermal paper, like that used in sales receipts.

Exposure to BPA causes fertility problems in women, impotence in men, and heart disease and other conditions in everyone.

Imagine you are a young girl given a plastic water bottle to take to school every day. BPA constantly leeches out into your system. If you don't detoxify estrogen well, you will get too much estrogen and become estrogen-toxic. That will lead to all sorts of developmental issues as you grow up.

## Environmental Toxins

People get exposed to many toxins daily, but standard blood tests don't reveal evidence. That's why a total toxicity test is so valuable for revealing what impacts people differently.

Everything goes back to what air you breathe, what you eat and drink, and the environment in which you live.

It's easy to dismiss these environmental issues as problems that mainly impact the less well-off. That's a myth. I'm here to tell you that most of my patients are not poor, but they still have problems with mold, substandard water, and inadequate food. No matter how wealthy we might be, we are all surrounded by harmful environmental factors. Companies frequently look to circumnavigate regulations by adding a preservative to food, releasing smoke or other gases into the air, or putting an additive into a textile, and all of those things can harm people. Women are impacted explicitly by female products, such as cosmetics, rinses, or moisturizers, that can disrupt their endocrine system.

I have my toxicology report done regularly. I have mold toxins because everyone in Texas gets exposed to mold. In addition, we have an older home with water leaks. Anywhere there's a moist environment, you'll get mold. The groundwater where I grew up was terrible, so I also have arsenic in my system, as well as parabens from plastics and shaving cream and glyphosates from foods grown with herbicides and pesticides.

It doesn't matter how much you wash food; some of the chemicals added to it as it is growing don't come off.

I also have sulfites (and more mold) from drinking wine. Any wine produced in the United States tends to have a lot of additives, so I prefer people to drink organic wine. Many of our alcoholic beverages are full of additives including ochratoxin, a mold toxin.

I wouldn't advise anyone not to drink alcohol, even though it makes sense. I just don't think they'd listen to me. Instead, I ask them to choose at least a better-quality drink, such as pure, filtered tequila or organic wine. You can always make choices; you just need to make the better ones as much as possible.

Before your procedure, we use our phase one detox program to prepare your body. After we test your toxicology, you can work with a detox practitioner for a four-to-six-week period to help reduce the toxins in your system. This also involves using supplements to improve the four key pathways we saw in the last chapter. Any genetic impairment of those pathways limits our body's ability to eliminate harmful toxins.

The toxicology report is often revelatory. People have a-ha moments when they realize that parts of their daily lives are increasing their toxic load and reducing their body's efficiency. This can be anything from their favorite snack to their walk along a busy road to work.

Once they have the results of the report, patients know that, whatever treatment they might be having, their recovery will not be hampered by toxins in their system without them realizing it.

Environmental toxins delay recovery on several levels, including limited stem cell activation and limitations in thyroid or sex hormone function. The result is that, overall, people remain swollen for longer after treatment. They have decreased energy levels, so their recovery will be slower.

Your toxic burden or exposure to toxins causes inflammation, which, as we saw in Chapter 1, affects every body system. Neural inflammation, cardiac inflammation, respiratory inflammation: Any kind of inflammation worsens over time with more exposure to toxicity.

When I talk to patients to determine how out of balance their systems are, I learn about their genetics and how toxins affect them. Many of the products we use daily affect a woman's endocrine system, ultimately affecting her mood, sleep, food and drink habits, and recovery.

If a woman feels anxious or tired and doesn't understand why, it's often because her endocrine system is off. Some substances we consume mimic the effects of estrogen, giving women phytoestrogen, which raises their hormone levels and makes them act in an unusual way.

Women naturally have more stress than men because they have higher levels of cortisol, which is associated with the fight-or-flight response. Men have more testosterone, which buffers out cortisol in their system. In addition, if women have more inflammation, they have even less of their good hormones, such as their thyroid or testosterone, to buffer out the bad hormones.

Many women instinctively know that something like this is true because it affects them. For many traditional medical practitioners, however, none of this makes sense. That's a concern because a disconnect has opened up between allopathic medicine and what we now call functional or integrative medicine. Again, patients know this and don't want to be limited by it. That's why they go in the millions to visit chiropractors, acupuncturists, homeopaths, and even psychics: They're trying to fill in the gaps left by so-called mainstream medicine.

## Chance to Change

We have an excellent opportunity to change things. This is a specific moment in time when we can blend all these traditions of medicine. I instinctively do it for my best interest, to enable my patients to get the best outcomes in surgery. Still, it's also perfectly aligned with what the medical profession should be doing. Consumers need to get over their big-brother fear of genetics, and health practitioners trained in the traditional Western canon need to see that alternative therapies can be objectively effective: we're not talking about faith healing or woo-woo nonsense here.

The data is the data. That's what I'd like to impress on my skeptical colleagues. Their only interest in any treatment should not be where it comes from but what the data show about it. Can we learn anything from it that might help us?

One way or another, we need to identify the exposures that cause inflammation and help patients detox. Only then can they have surgery, whatever type of surgery it is.

We use a toxicology test to establish a baseline that provides a jumping-off point to put patients through inflammation-lowering diets, detoxification programs with supplements of different formulations, or therapeutic services such as infrared sauna.

The danger is this: someone has a treatment where the surgeon in the operating room is pleased with the result because everything looks good, but the patient then stays swollen for a long time because of their toxins. If they've detoxed, the swelling will go away sooner.

As the surgical recovery program gains popularity, everyone will prepare for treatment in the same way. That will help recovery become more uniform—and that, in turn, might reduce patient dissatisfaction.

CHAPTER 4

# Food

The overall aim of the surgical recovery program is to remove all the things from your life that limit your body's ability to function optimally. Everything starts with your diet. Don't put anything into the engine that will make it run at a less efficient pace.

Everyone knows the importance of eating well, so I won't say too much about it other than organizing your diet is critical.

It's worth noting that the modifications humans have made to food in terms of how we grow, process, store, and prepare it make much of the stuff we eat potentially harmful to us. It triggers inflammation, leads to problems such as endocrine dysfunction, which affects the thyroid and sex hormones, and screws up our immune system.

That slows down recovery.

When it needs to heal, your body sends signals and cells to start the inflammatory process. If all your metabolic activity is in lockstep, you heal. If there are distractions in other areas or your cells can't activate, reach their targets, or be effective, you'll stay swollen longer. You need to get your body in the right state for optimum results. In particular, you need your white blood cells, which fight illness and promote recovery, functioning optimally.

Your basic cellular functions will fail if you can't absorb vitamins and minerals. Those nutrients usually come from food, although they can be provided intravenously if someone has had gastrointestinal surgery.

Your gut has to work to absorb nutrients from food. However, as we'll see in the next chapter, many things prevent it from working well. These include taking too many antibiotics or other medications such as Accutane, but they mainly revolve around eating low-quality food that has additives or that contains herbicides and pesticides.

To enhance recovery, your diet needs to contain food of a high enough quality that it can give you the vitamins and minerals you need. That means whole fruits and vegetables and grass-fed, non-hormone-grown animals. It might mean a largely or entirely vegetarian diet, but it shouldn't mean a vegan diet. Vegan diets almost always include too much soy and processed food, which you should avoid to reduce inflammation and increase detoxification.

You might think, "Why not tell us to go to Whole Foods and buy organic produce?"

Well, that wouldn't be a bad way to start. Organic produce and meat are better if *organic* means not grown or raised without fertilizers, antibiotics, or artificial hormones. It's worth bearing in mind that the entire food-labeling industry has become so misleading and tangled up in bureaucracy that even products labeled as organic can contain so many harmful ingredients they are worse for you than non-organic food.

So, I do recommend organic food, but only if it's truly organic. The best approach is to eat fresh fruit and vegetables that haven't been sprayed with insecticides and herbicides as if you could go to the farm and pick them yourself.

It will be good for you if it's fresh and organic, whether a potato, tomato, corn, or citrus fruit like orange or nectarine. Fresh fruit and vegetables are the best way to get sugar and carbs. Our ancestors didn't eat flour, and any fat they ate came from eating the meat of dead animals. You'd never see an obese caveman because the diet had no extra carbs. The paleo diet is based on whatever cavemen would have been able to forage for or hunt.

When it comes to meat, eat grass-fed, pasture-raised farm animals whenever possible. Many farm animals in the United States are mass-raised and fed hormones and antibiotics. When my son used to play soccer against teams from the Midwest, the opposition players were often 20 or 30 pounds heavier. It's potentially because they're consuming additional hormones in the meat they eat and the milk they drink. Those hormones and antibiotics affect people's endocrine system, which means that males get gynecomastia at a very high rate because hormones in food make them produce too much estrogen.

## Food and Nutrition

The nutritional value of the food we should eat is more complex.

Most people know they should eat around 2,000 calories daily to be healthy—but we should be wary of such a broad guideline. That figure doesn't have as much science behind it as you might think. Nutritionists created it in the seventies before we knew as much as we know about differences between individuals and their nutrition needs. We now understand that individuals' specific genetics dictate how they metabolize carbs, fats, and proteins. That means there's no way a nutritionist can just tell someone to eat 2,000 calories in whatever balance they like without knowing their genetic profile. Suppose a person has a non-celiac gluten sensitivity and eats carbohydrates with white flour or bread. In that case, they won't lose weight, even if they stick religiously to the total calories.

Rather than being guided by a spurious calorie intake, I advise people to eat well.

When patients come to my clinic in Austin, I give them all a gift card for a restaurant named The Well, which serves some of the healthiest food in the city (www.eatwellatx.com). The food is all organic and has no supplements or additives. The menu excludes gluten, seed oils, soy, refined sugar, GMOs, or dairy. That makes it the ideal food to eat to prepare for a treatment. It's also revelatory for patients who would never naturally associate eating healthily with delicious food.

As you prepare for your procedure at home, try a lower-carbohydrate, higher-protein diet, including healthier types of fat, avocados, oily fish, and suitable oils and seeds. You shouldn't eat white bread, cake, or cookies. If you want something sweet, eat fruit or vegetables—but watch out for those that contain lots of sugar.

Even if you don't know the nutritional value of particular types of food, it's not complicated to hack your diet. Cutting out gluten and dairy and eliminating processed foods will have a transformational effect. That's especially true if you also exercise.

It's easy to find apps to help you count macros in your diet, meaning how much fat, carbohydrate, and protein you are eating, and simply understanding that gives you information to make better decisions, which empowers you to take more control over your health. Anyone can use the camera on their phone to scan what they eat in a macro-counting app and become more aware of where there are problems and where they can make changes. That can help narrow the gap between what medical advice tells them to do and how they live. I'm all for that. Like the rest of the surgical recovery program, it's all about execution to get the performance we want.

We have specific guidance on diet. You might find that strange for a plastic surgeon, but because diet is one of the foundations of a successful recovery, it's worth having a specialist on hand to advise patients. People can easily make themselves sick by eating the wrong foods or can become confused by instructions such as cutting out gluten, so helping educate them about that is a massive part of making sure they're ready for treatment.

A bad diet is one of the most challenging things to correct. Many of us were raised on low-quality, sugary soda and candy, and switching to a healthy diet can be difficult. (Another genetic response is why some kids act crazy when they eat so many sugary snacks. They can't metabolize sugar, so it stays in their system longer and gives them neural inflammation.)

## Trace Minerals

A healthy metabolism and immune system depend on seven trace minerals the body needs: iron, manganese, copper, iodine, zinc, cobalt, fluoride, and selenium. These substances are necessary for proper enzymatic function at the cellular level. You'll be familiar with many, such as zinc, iron, and selenium, but others, like manganese, might be less well known. You can get most of them from a healthy diet, particularly meat, fish, vegetables, and nuts. We get iron from eating meat, for example, so if you're a vegetarian, you'll likely lack some iron.

It is challenging to get enough trace elements from our food, mainly cobalt, so I include them in my supplements.

There's a danger with supplements that the more you have to take, the more compliance goes down. My supplements are designed for you to take indefinitely. Once they help you feel better, I want you to feel even better by continuing to take them. You should never want to stop things because you should become addicted to how it feels and always like to make yourself feel better.

CHAPTER 5

# The Gut Microbiome

This chapter is about how our gut works. You might wonder whether it needs to be separate from the chapter about food and diet, given that the two are so closely related, but the gut gets its chapter because it's vital for the whole central nervous system (CNS). The axis linking the gut to the brain is one of the most critical physiological relationships in the body because it helps control our central nervous system—and thus enables a healthy recovery. The gut directly impacts the brain's health and ability to control the CNS.

We each have about 100 trillion microbes in our stomachs that comprise our gut microbiome. This collection of tiny bacteria and fungi is necessary to digest our food, breaking it down and extracting the nutrition we need to support our body by getting energy to our cells through sugars and carbohydrates. However, the gut microbiome is finely balanced, and any shift in the balance can cause dysfunction. For example, you would have more gas if you had more methane-producing bacteria. If you have an imbalance in h pylori, you might be more at risk of inflammation or ulcers.

The gut is at the heart of digestion. That's the process by which our body absorbs nutrients from the food and drink we consume, reclaims the water, and eliminates the waste as poop or pee. When your gut microbiome is out of balance, it limits your ability to absorb nutrients, so your body doesn't get all the nutrients it needs. You may be more constipated, which will determine your ability to eliminate waste and detoxify your body from harmful substances. If you can't poop, those substances build up in your body.

Preparing for treatment involves making our gut better take advantage of the nutrition we're giving it. That requires that the gut lining be intact, with no bacterial or fungal imbalance that lessens its effectiveness. The basis for that goes back to eating and drinking the right things rather than eating bread or swilling beer.

As we age, our enzymatic capacity decreases. Digestive enzymes are the proteins that break down our food into proteins, carbohydrates, sugars, and fats, so this decline means we can extract fewer nutrients from our food. Again, that's something we need to counteract to achieve maximum efficiency in the gut.

When the gut microbiome is out of balance, we suffer from intolerances triggered by specific foods.

Imagine, for example, that you go with friends to an Italian restaurant that has nothing but five-star reviews, and you have a plate of pasta. It tastes delicious, but you don't feel too good afterward—though everyone with you feels great. The chances are that you have a gluten sensitivity without realizing it, and the gluten in the pasta has triggered you. Your body interprets the gluten as a signal to your gut to produce inflammation. Your stomach will swell, and you'll look and feel puffy.

Your gut has the most lymphatic tissue in your body, and that tissue reacts to food intolerance. In my case, my gut is triggered by gluten, eggs, and sunflower oil. (Sunflower oil is commonly used for potato chips, so I can only eat chips made with avocado oil.)

If I eat those triggers, I put on 10 pounds. If I stop eating them, I lose it again. Anyone who identified their triggers and then avoided them would lose 10 pounds in fluid alone because what we eat and drink produces fluid that causes swelling and edema, which is the medical name for the inflammation that makes us puffy.

If you eliminate the things that trigger your gut, so you're only eating food to which you don't have a sensitivity, your gut will work better, and you will absorb better. That will ensure you get the nutrition your brain, cells, heart, and lungs need.

Having the right balance in the gut microbiome doesn't only maximize our absorptive capacity. It also makes it easier to detoxify. Toxins only leave the body through urine, sweat, and poop. You can't eliminate them that way if you don't exercise or sweat. If you don't poop more than once a day, you're not getting rid of them quickly enough.

It all comes down to your absorptive capacity relative to your elimination capacity. In other words, eating low-quality food and upsetting your gut microbiome will affect your detoxification ability. If you're constipated and you don't sweat, then you can only pee, which means you have only a limited ability to detoxify.

One popular way for people to try to help their gut is by taking probiotics, which are living yeasts and bacteria intended to supplement your gut microbiome. Probiotics are often beneficial, but sometimes, people who take them feel gut pain. If that happens, it's a sign that they have upset the balance of their gut microbiome. A probiotic can intensify the action of methane-producing bacteria. That causes pain because you produce more gas, and the intestinal wall expands, creating pressure and pain until you go to the bathroom. Probiotics *can* help balance out your gut—but if you don't know what's wrong with your gut microbiome before you start, adding probiotics can risk making it worse.

Virtually everyone who comes to my clinic has a gut microbiome imbalance, and most don't even realize it. That's a concern because gut microbiome imbalance has many downstream effects. It affects the gut-brain axis and inhibits the four immune system pathways.

Our solution is to have detox specialists who work on getting the patients' gut to bind better with toxins so the toxins can be passed out of the body. At the same time, we provide liquid supplements that can bypass the gut entirely, ensuring important substances can get into the body even if your gut's absorptive ability is low.

Once test results confirm the imbalance, our detox partners work with patients to correct their gut microbiome. They study all of the patient's test results and devise a supplement route for a phase one detox based on whether the patient needs a mold detox, a heavy metal detox, or is dealing with an environmental toxin. We have supplements specifically formulated to help overcome each specific problem.

The supplements we use to reduce inflammation are mostly liquid-based, so they're formulated to be absorbed in the oral cavity in your mouth and avoid the gut. It takes away any excuses from people who are reluctant to take more pills. It's easy to get pill fatigue because people don't like taking them, so we try to eliminate that danger.

In the words of my old friend, Dr. Adam Poole, "I don't want to hear excuses. I just want improvement."

The B vitamins, C vitamins, glutathione, and vitamin D3 + K2 in my inflammation support bundle come as liquids. They are the principal elements you need for function at the cellular level. In addition, there is magnesium powder, a carnitine tablet for detox, and a tablet known as CDG for mitochondrial function.

That is the best way to limit lousy inflammation for people about to have treatment.

It's a process I wish we could use to set up all cosmetic surgery patients worldwide for success. The playbook is universal: your genetics, your diet, your toxins, your poop. Get those right, and your recovery will be quicker.

CHAPTER 6

# Hormones

As we've seen, everyone has too much inflammation. That means nearly everyone has problems with their thyroid, which is the first thing inflammation affects.

The thyroid gland is in your throat. It regulates our hormones through the endocrine system, which controls our growth and development. The thyroid governs our metabolism, which helps to regulate our temperature. If people are hypothyroid, they get cold quickly; if they're hyperthyroid, they feel warm and may have higher heart rates.

In general the thyroid seems to be very sensitive to inflammation. That can cause changes in their metabolism that lead them to gain weight. When people are younger, sculpting their appearance by working out or adjusting their diet is usually quite manageable. As they age, their hormones throw off their endocrine system; however, controlling body shape through exercise or diet is far more difficult because the thyroid is not working correctly.

Your brain and endocrine organs need nutrition to make hormones, so restoring your hormone balance starts with whatever you put in your mouth. The basic premise we've already seen remains: cut out gluten, cut out dairy, cut out processed foods, and cut out sugars that don't come from natural sources such as berries. If you do that, your endocrine organs will work better.

Once your thyroid becomes inefficient, you feel like you have less energy. You can't lose weight or sculpt yourself. This is due to your sex hormones, estrogen, progesterone, and testosterone, coupled with the stress hormone cortisol.

People who have endocrine dysfunction typically have such high inflammation that their thyroid doesn't function well, and they become hypothyroid. This doesn't always show up in lab tests and bloodwork, but if you're female and constantly stressed out, it's likely because your cortisol is high. Your estrogen may also be super high, so you have too much estrogen and cortisol. Your cortisol burns out from adrenal fatigue, which leads to a lack of production of sex hormones. That leaves you feeling bad because you have low thyroid function and metabolism. You have too much estrogen, which causes stress and anxiety. They give women bad cycle pain, so they have cramps and can't go to work.

Estrogen is also responsible for endometriosis, polycystic ovarian syndrome, and other adverse outcomes. If you have too much inflammation, it may be that you also have completely suppressed testosterone levels, or your estrogen may be super high (progesterone is a pregnancy hormone, so it's usually less critical). In lab tests, your testosterone may be so suppressed that it looks like it's not even there.

I'm less interested in lab results with my patients than how a woman feels. Usually, she feels terrible all the time. If a woman has a low thyroid number, many doctors put her on thyroid medicine or synthetic hormones. But when I ask those women, "Does that make you feel better? Can you notice a difference?" the answer in most cases is that it's hard to tell.

The women aren't getting better because their inflammation is so high that the synthetic hormone can't get to work to help their metabolism.

Men have more testosterone, which helps buffer out estrogen and super-high cortisol. That's why males are usually less inclined to anxiety than women. When men suffer from low testosterone, however, they sometimes become more anxious and have more fatigue, especially if they're more estrogen-dominant in their metabolism.

My goal with any hormone treatment is to help provide balance. I don't put people on thyroid medicine. Once we alter a patient's diet and move them onto our anti-inflammatory supplements, inflammation reduces, and their thyroid and other hormones work better. We use hormone supplements to increase a woman's baseline testosterone level and help balance out their estrogen. We also have synthetic hormone supplementation with testosterone pellet therapy.

Sometimes, such as when a woman has old breast implants, there's too much inflammation to be able to correct it purely through diet and supplements. You need a large enough dose of hormone so that it can battle through the inflammation to get to the target and affect it.

Some of my patients have already tried hormone therapy and complained that it didn't work. I tell them there are only two ways drugs like synthetic hormones don't work: You're either not taking them correctly, or you're not taking enough of them.

I ask them many questions: Did your hair and nail growth improve? Did your energy level improve? Did your focus improve? Did your libido improve? If the answer to all those is no, then once again, either their inflammation is too high, or the dose is too low.

The issue for a medical practitioner is whether to give them enough hormones to battle the current level of inflammation or whether to work beforehand to reduce their inflammation and help them get the most benefit. At my clinic, we try to lower their inflammation to a stage where their genetic capability for hormone production, or synthetic replacements, can benefit them.

I don't replace estrogen and progesterone, just testosterone, which helps recovery. That can present a challenge for women, who need very little testosterone. An average male may need 1,200 milligrams of testosterone, which comes as either a pellet or a shot. That's simple. A female needs precisely one-twelfth of that. Giving that as a pellet that dissolves over four months is quite simple, but giving it in a shot is less precise. In many cases women have not received the correct amount.

Some doctors are too relaxed about this. They give a woman the same bottle of testosterone they would provide a man and don't tell them how much to inject. I don't allow any injectable testosterone to be administered to women. It's too hard to control.

(I don't give anybody progesterone, by the way, because no one ever tells you that its number one side effect is constipation. Women often complain anyway about bowel issues, such as bloating, swelling, or constipation, because they have stress-related problems with their GI tract, so giving them progesterone will only make things worse. Some people take it to help them sleep, but there are many other, better ways to sleep that don't mean you wake up constipated.)

## Peptides

You might have heard of a particular type of a combination of amino acids called peptides, which some athletes use to help their bodies recover after exercise. They're something of a fashion at the moment, but I don't put my patients on peptide therapy. Many of my patients are hesitant about needles, and many peptides have to be self-injected, not ingested. That makes it highly unlikely a patient will go through with a complete treatment anyway.

Peptides are smaller versions of proteins known as precursors. One study in particular looked at BPC-157, which helps in recovery. As I've said, many athletes are using it. I started trying peptides several years ago to see how they worked.

It's one of my fundamental principles that I would never give anyone anything I hadn't tried. I have to understand the physiological effect a therapy will have on somebody, good or bad.

Some peptides stimulate growth hormone, which is only secreted at night. Taking them one hour before bed will help your HRV, improve your sleep, and boost your growth hormone production.

We only recover when we sleep. That's when the trash gets taken out of your brain, and recovery happens because our lymphatic system can deal with the depressurized, horizontal person, not someone like me with swollen legs from standing all day in the operating room.

I don't give patients peptide therapies. There can be side effects, plus there's a danger that someone gives themselves an infection if they contaminate themselves while they're injecting it.

If you want to find out more, I've added a list of the most common peptides and their benefits at the end of the book.

PART II

# TREATMENT

CHAPTER 7

# The Treatment

As we saw in the first part of the book, your recovery starts long before you have any treatment. As soon as you decide that you'd like to have a procedure done and you book yourself in, you can take the genetic and toxicity tests. Then, you start working with my staff to go through the phase-one detox process and begin a course of our supplements to reduce inflammation as much as possible.

Remember, we'll cause a lot more inflammation during treatment.

It's just like training for a sports tournament: you've got to prepare for the event. When you fly into Austin to visit the clinic the day before the treatment, you've done all the work. Now, you just have to execute.

The time immediately before treatment can be challenging. Many people get stressed out and anxious, especially if they've had a negative experience from a painful augmentation or they've had other operations that haven't gone well. Unfortunately, that's not uncommon in paid-for treatments. Patients may have post-traumatic stress that floods their bodies with cortisol, making them super-tense.

We reassure them about why the program is successful. We remind them that they've put the work in to prepare themselves for recovery by altering their lifestyle and diet, and they've gotten used to taking the inflammation-lowering supplements. We remind them there's a game plan in place, with a team in the operating room and a team at my office. We review the surgery plan and answer any questions they might have. We send them to The Well to have a delicious meal containing no harmful ingredients. We also put them on specific medications the night before treatment to decrease inflammation, calm the nervous system, and help them sleep.

It's not unusual for my patients to have a high psychological and emotional burden. I'm used to it, so I can help them keep it in perspective. Throughout my career, I've dealt with cancer patients who are worried about dying and leaving their kids or spouses alone; each patient goes through stress like that.

For cosmetic treatment, we aim to get patients into a parasympathetic state. To understand that, we need to start with our autonomic nervous system, which controls bodily functions, and we need to be conscious of them, such as breathing, blood circulation, and digestion. The autonomic nervous system has two main modes: the sympathetic and parasympathetic responses.

The sympathetic response is our fight-or-flight mechanism. The parasympathetic response restores us to safe energy.

What's the difference? Imagine you go on safari, and a lion gets too close to your jeep. Your heart would race, your pupils would dilate, and your blood vessels would constrict in your gut and shunt blood to the muscles in your limbs so you can run faster to get out of there. Your digestive system would shut down to save energy. That's the sympathetic response kicking in. It all happens without you being conscious of it.

It's the opposite of the relaxed, parasympathetic state. We can help ourselves achieve the parasympathetic state in many ways, such as doing tai chi or chi gong, meditation, yoga, listening to music, or walking.

I see the sympathetic response in patients who don't look me in the eye and are twitchy and on edge. They become so stressed it's hard for them to say, "Okay, I'm ready for my treatment." They need the surgical recovery program more than most people because their autonomic nervous system is off-track, which probably means that other things are off-track, too.

As we saw earlier, this can be worse in women who don't handle the sympathetic nervous system response well because they have more estrogen, which makes it worse. In males, testosterone helps buffer out some of the fight-or-flight response.

People who are this stressed day over day, week over week, month over month, feel as if they have pain moving around everywhere. One day, it'll be in their neck. The next day, it'll be in their calf. The next day, it'll be in their hand. Once you're like that, the pain just keeps moving around. It seems as if they're crazy, but they're not.

They're not making the pain up. It's what doctors call ischemic pain. The blood vessels constrict and reduce oxygen flow to the muscle, causing pain. It's just that the person's mind activates their autonomic nervous system in precisely the same way as they would if they saw the lion. That can be terrifying.

One patient told me she started getting pain in her calf as if a horse had kicked her. It was a year after her daughter was born. That was a sign. Young children are stressors, so her autonomic nervous system has kicked in.

The best way to help someone with an overstimulated autonomic nervous system is to put them in an oxygen-rich environment. I have a pressurized hyperbaric chamber in my clinic that provides exactly that. So many physical and mental issues come down to a lack of oxygen. Anyone who spends time inside the chamber feels better afterward because everyone's brain works better with more oxygen. Even if you don't sleep well and everything hurts, more oxygen will make you feel better. Some top athletes sleep in hyperbaric chambers at night to help them recover from training.

Additional oxygen helps put patients in a parasympathetic mindset less invasively than other methods, such as hallucinogens. The parasympathetic system reverses the process activated by the sympathetic system. It constricts the pupils, decreases the heart rate, and restores digestion. It lowers blood pressure and diverts blood back to the skin and the digestive tract. The parasympathetic system conserves energy and soothes the mind and body.

By the morning of the treatment, most of my patients are in a parasympathetic state as long as they've followed the protocol, which can be difficult for people who are control freaks because they have to trust the process. They're calm and well-rested because of the medication we give them to help them sleep. Some tell me they've enjoyed their best sleep in years.

We don't put people in a parasympathetic state just because it's more pleasant for them. It's also much easier for an anesthetist to put people who are already relaxed to sleep without having to give them an excess of narcotics to bring down their heart rate and blood pressure. That removes any risk of overmedication by the anesthetist during the treatment because a lot of medication is simply unnecessary.

The anesthetist's goal is to put you to sleep so you're unaware of what's going on. People are sometimes anxious about waking up during the treatment. Maybe they've heard horror stories about that happening. None of my patients have ever woken up. There's no reason they would because we only use anesthesia to complement the body's natural state.

## Aiding Recovery

Enhanced Recovery after Surgery, or ERAS, is a basic protocol across all surgical disciplines. It's intended to be the standard of care for everybody around the world who has a surgical procedure, and it's increasingly widely adopted, even though it goes against some forms of established surgical practice. In many ways, it's the foundation of the surgical recovery program. It concentrates on maintaining good organ function, optimizing nutrition, using standardized regimes for anesthetics and painkillers, and getting patients moving as soon after treatment as possible.

I'm a big supporter of ERAS, but the surgical recovery program differs in one crucial way. We start things sooner than the ERAS protocol suggests. We do as much as we can *before* treatment or problems develop so that we don't get stuck in simply reacting to how someone is recovering.

One small example. Most clinics give patients medication to relax them just before treatment. That doesn't provide the medication time to work, so we have our patients take them the evening before their treatment.

Everything we do is before, not after. We proactively treat any source of discomfort. When I remove a breast implant, for example, I use an injection to numb the ribs, muscular tissues, soft tissues, skin, fat, and breast tissue. It's similar to the injection you get in your mouth from the dentist, but in this case, the numbing effect lasts about a week.

After the treatment, we wrap patients with an ace wrap for compression, with ice between the layers of the wrap. If a top athlete sprains their ankle, they put an ice bag on them because ice is still the best anti-inflammatory in the world. It reduces the external and internal swelling caused by the treatment.

When sports doctors treat injuries, they follow a protocol known as RICE: rest, ice, compression, and elevation. In many ways, our post-treatment approach is the same. We make sure the patient rests well in a stress-free environment. We use ice to reduce inflammation. We compress the area around the treatment using dressings. And we elevate the affected part of the body as much as possible (although this is not always practicable).

When the patient wakes up, depending on how long the treatment has lasted, the affected part of their body will continue to be numb and, in the case of an explant, will get more numb. They could leave the surgery center within 30 to 40 minutes if we let them. However, it's our protocol that they have to go in a wheelchair, just as an additional precaution.

Patients can eat and drink normally for the rest of the day if they feel like it. However, they may have some sensitivity to the anesthetic gas, which could make them feel nauseated and not like eating. In any case, I recommend they only have lighter food, such as a smoothie or juice, until the evening. If they take it easy on the first day, they can resume a more normal diet the next day.

People who have had bad experiences with paid-for medical treatment are often pleasantly surprised. In some cases, they've had treatments that have caused stress and trauma, and they subconsciously expect the experience in my clinic to be the same. It's not. I've been improving how I do this for many years, and it's a relatively straightforward treatment. I can't speak for what happens with other surgeons, but there's no reason any paid-for treatment should ever be a bad experience for the patient. We all can do better.

I'd add one observation, however. The rise in social media has done nothing to help people prepare for treatment. Social media has created what is almost completely a highly negative environment around paid-for treatments—and indeed around all types of medicine. If I could, I would stop my patients from looking at it. From an emotional standpoint, it doesn't put people in the right mindset. Instead, it generates unnecessary fear about very standard and safe procedures.

It's difficult for people to get reliable medical information in this environment. They don't usually have access to peer-reviewed academic journals, where my team and I get our information. Even if they did, they wouldn't necessarily understand the articles because they can be highly technical. After all, they are written for people with years of experience and a solid foundation of knowledge.

One of the reasons I'm writing this book is to provide an accessible source of reliable information about cosmetic treatment. I would much rather people get their information from me than from asking Google or, even worse, from Facebook.

PART III

# AFTER THE TREATMENT

CHAPTER 8

# The First Week

Depending on your exact treatment, you may feel discomfort on the first day or two after treatment. That should only last until the nerve-blocking medication has had time to work. A little oral pain medication will help you through that initial period, and then you need very little narcotic at all.

Some people are eager to get rid of the pain medicine as soon as possible. They say, "I don't want to take it." They're more worried about becoming addicted or not feeling themselves than they are about avoiding discomfort. Other people worry about being able to get hold of schedule two drugs when they go home, as I can't prescribe across state lines, so they can only follow the protocol while they're in Texas.

Take it from me. No one is going to get addicted to pain medication the way we help them recover. I make people remain on an anti-inflammatory and their medications for one simple reason: it works. I've had enough surgeries myself to know what happens when pain medicine wears off.

## Visiting the Clinic

On the first day, at a minimum, you'll come in for treatments to reduce any excess fluids created by the treatment. If you've had breast treatment, for example, the IV fluids we use during surgery drain into the tissues in your torso. We need to reduce that excess fluid, which we do by using the body's lymphatic system. That's part of your immune system that usually moves fluids around your body, so we're leveraging the best filtration system in the world.

In the clinic, we have unique devices that use pressure to drain excess fluids from the entire lower two-thirds of the body. They can also drain the whole body, if necessary.

You'll also have light-based therapy in which you sit in front of a 6-foot red light for 10 minutes. Red light therapy is quite a recent treatment that emerged from experiments in the 1990s. NASA scientists found that red light encouraged plants to grow and helped any cuts and scrapes the scientists had to heal more quickly. Red light is known to decrease inflammation and help with pain control (it also has many other effects, such as optimizing athletic performance and optimizing hormone function). As we've seen, the more we can decrease inflammation, the more your immune system can focus on recovery from treatment.

The following day, you come in for hyperbaric therapy. We put you in a chamber with pure oxygen pressurized at about 1.3 to 1.5 atmospheres. Our upright tank is easy to get in and out of and comfortable to sit inside. You can listen to music, answer emails or texts, or read a book.

Oxygen helps everyone. It allows you to clear anesthesia quickly. It reduces inflammation and brain fog in people who don't detox well. When tissues have been damaged, people who are healing need more nutrition and oxygen. The hyperbaric chamber helps provide oxygen.

None of this is rocket science. Oxygen is good for you, so we just give you more at a time when your body needs more. My treatment generally relies on providing what the body wants: more nutrients, protein, and supplementation because recovery needs Vitamin C and D, B vitamins, and glutathione. (We sort out all the supplements for you, although you can find them online, too, under the brand name Dr Rob's Solutions.)

Everything is set up for you to achieve the outcome.

## Starting Your Recovery

The rest of the week, you concentrate on your rest and apply ice to the treatment area. Most protocols recommend 20 minutes on and 20 minutes off for ice, but we have found that people soon get tired of that. It's easier to aim to do it fewer times. We prefer 30 minutes on and 30 minutes off.

You come to the office daily for treatments so we can ensure that you eat, drink, and rest.

Typically, a week after the treatment, I will see you to check if the surgical sites are acceptable, although I know they always are. There are no external stitches. When the treatment is over, we glue everything shut and cover it with a transparent dressing that protects the wound but still allows us to see if there are any problems.

Patients will continue to use ice for the first two weeks at the surgical sites. I encourage all patients to start walking as soon as possible but not to lift anything heavier than a heavy bag of groceries. It's not time to go back to lifting weights. Also, you're on narcotics, which means no driving and no operating heavy machinery.

You can leave Austin and continue your recovery at home at the end of the first week. After a couple more weeks, there's just a little clear bandage that you can take off yourself at home.

No sutures can be removed because all the stitches are underneath the skin. Subcutaneous stitches don't leave any little knots sticking out that can increase scarring. Then we use skin glue that acts as a waterproof barrier, with a clear bandage on top to ensure it can't be damaged by a fingernail, rubbed by your clothes, or brushed against anything else. The glue adds a bit of tensile strength to hold things together.

We do everything we can to limit scarring, but with some treatments, such as breast reshaping or removing implants, some scarring is inevitable. With minimally invasive body contouring, there's little to no scarring. With many treatments, such as if I take fat out of somebody's love handles, abdomen, or inner or outer thighs, the openings in the skin are only 3 millimeters long.

CHAPTER 9

# Following Up

After the first week, your next appointment with my team is at one month and then approximately 90 days. By then, most of the swelling will have disappeared from even the most extensive procedures.

We see most often at the 90-day stage that the patient's overall well-being is typically better. They've gotten through the most challenging aspects of recovery. Their energy levels are better because they're taking the supplements. They are feeling more like themselves, and they've resumed some exercise. They will have started light exercise at six weeks, probably using their body weight to do air squats or lunges. Exercise increases dopamine, so they're feeling better. Everybody likes a little dopamine to help them feel happier.

If you've had body contouring, you're getting used to your new shape. If you were a size four dress, you're getting used to being a two. If you were a two, you love being a zero.

At 90 days, there are a lot of pluses.

At this stage, patients might ask, "Can I stop taking supplements?" When they say that, I ask them, "Do you feel good?" When they say yes, I ask them, "Well if you feel good taking supplements, why wouldn't the question be, how can I still feel better? Is there something else I can take to make me feel better consistently?"

Suppose the surgical recovery program has helped you feel better about achieving your goals daily, taking care of your family, doing your work, and keeping a good energy level throughout the day. Why would you want to stop it? You should be thinking, "I've got better energy levels and more focus naturally by leveraging my genetics, my diet, and my supplementation."

About two weeks after surgery, patients start phase one of our detox program. The organs get overloaded by the toxins we take in from our food and our environment, so we use supplements to help open up drainage pathways in the body to support cellular health. We give patients minerals to give the body the energy it needs to heal. We also use binders to start binding up toxins in the body, making it easier to eliminate them.

Phase two of our detox focuses on digestive health. We use supplements to clean the gut of toxins and biofilm, the protective mechanism that viruses, bacteria, fungi, and parasites secrete that protects them from our immune system.

If you give antimicrobials to someone without breaking down their biofilm, it's challenging to target the infection entirely. We pair antimicrobials that will work on the infection with biofilm busters that allow the antimicrobials to get to where they can work best. Meanwhile, we support the body with minerals and binders to bind up the toxins so that we can pull them out of the system.

People sometimes tell me, "I'd prefer not to take the supplements. I'll get what the supplements give me from my food instead." To be honest, most people couldn't afford to eat the quality or amount of food it would take to get the same benefits you gain from the supplements.

I tell people, "If you think supplements are expensive, why don't you try hiring a private chef who can cook five-star food in the appropriate oils for every meal?" They would soon see how much cheaper my program is than that one.

The truth is, the stuff I told you to do in part one of the book, which was the pre-treatment preparation for a quick recovery—genetics, food, toxicology, gut microbiome, and so on—is a great way just to carry on living. It's a playbook for life because it maximizes your body's ability to do everything it's supposed to do.

You only have one body, so if the surgical recovery program helps it perform better, why would you not continue with it? If you told a professional athlete you had a surefire, natural way to get them 1 percent better at their event, any of them would jump at the chance.

It's what coaches call a marginal gains perspective. It's all about performance.

You have to trust the program. Ideally, you'll get addicted to feeling the right way, so you'll want to stick to it rather than give it up. I don't understand why people find it challenging to maintain and lose a little desire to follow through—because I do all this myself. I take a whole range of supplements myself. I do hormone therapy, hyperbaric oxygen therapy, and lymphatic massage therapy.

I'm trying to hack into the best version of myself, and I want to help you, too. I'm always looking for new techniques that will help.

## Six and Nine Months

At six months, I meet with clients who need help with their initial evaluation and detoxification process. The surgery is usually fine by now, but I check patients quarterly to see if they have other problems. (Most surgeons don't check in after the first month).

Most of our patients have moved on to another phase of our detox program.

Phase three addresses toxins in the whole body. Pathogens and toxins often travel from the digestive tract into other organ systems, so this phase targets the immune system and organs such as the heart, brain, kidneys, or liver. We focus on binding toxins in the body, which come from chemicals in food and the environment and viruses within the body. We use particular types of binders to help get rid of the toxins.

In phase four, we address the less severe bacteria and fungi in the body. They're not massively harmful, but they are present because they've been allowed to establish themselves by the presence of more prominent pathogens, such as H pylori, or by severe bacterial overgrowth. When we clean up those more prominent pathogens, focusing on tiny bacteria, fungi, and yeast overgrowth is easier. Many of our patients have mold and fungus issues, so phase four uses a specific binder to clean up any heavy metals and environmental toxins.

## Twelve Months

Many patients find that their overall health has improved since they started following the SHARP program and want to continue enjoying the benefits. After they finish being surgical patients, they transition to our wellness practice based in my Austin clinic and apply many SHARP principles to daily life to help them achieve the best versions of themselves.

If people still have physical problems due to their procedure, such as body contouring that hasn't fully tightened up, we'll already address them. More often, there are few physical issues at this stage.

Our wellness practice is holistic. It supports the individual with positive lifestyle and diet changes and supplementation to help improve their body's key pathways. This ensures they can continue detoxing effectively and gain the nutrition they need to minimize their chronic inflammation.

Anyone following the SHARP protocols is likely to lose weight, feel more energetic, and be generally healthier, so we encourage all our patients to continue on the holistic path they started to prepare for their procedure and recovery. Many don't need much encouragement, having experienced the benefits for themselves. Since their procedure, they've felt less stressed and more energized because we've helped them reduce inflammation through detoxification and balancing their genetic makeup with better nutrition and supplementation.

I know how difficult it is to get someone to change their behavior, so we provide as much support as people need. We run total toxicity tests and constantly monitor the results and the quality of their food choices. If someone struggles to make the right choices, we can offer support and advice at every step.

A year after your procedure, you'll be aware of two changes. First, your body shape is now what you wanted it to be. By now, the effects of the procedure have become part of your vision of yourself that inspired you to take action in the first place. That's a permanent change. Second, you're feeling healthier, have more energy, and your mood is more stable because you have less inflammation and less toxicity.

There's no reason that can't be a permanent change if you transition to joining our wellness practice.

You've already been living better on the SHARP recovery scheme. Why stop now?

PART IV

# THE FUTURE

CHAPTER 10

# What's Next?

There's a reason I've got $3 million of medical equipment in my office to help patients kickstart their recovery, including my unique lymphatic device and the hyperbaric chamber. Medicine is constantly advancing, and I'm excited to keep up with technology that I think will benefit my patients because, in benefiting them, it also helps me.

It's an exciting time for therapy. Medical procedures are emerging that have the potential to revolutionize cosmetic treatment and recovery. Take plasmapheresis, in which practitioners remove blood plasma from a patient, filter it in a machine, and then return it to the bloodstream. It's a valuable way we might be able to combat autoimmune diseases. Plasmapheresis is already a fairly standard procedure in Europe, but it's only now gaining popularity in the United States.

## Stem Cell Therapy

One of the devices I use processes stem cells, one of the most promising new therapies. You've probably come across stem cell therapy in the media because, a few years ago, it was the subject of some fear-mongering stories about mad scientists being able to create humans without procreation. Those stories had no scientific basis. They were based more on ethical arguments about the right to life than on understanding stem cells.

Stem cells are simply the body's baseline cells: blank cells that can develop into any specialized cells the body needs as it grows or repairs itself. That means they are fantastic for helping people recover after treatment.

There's no better juice than your genetic material.

Medical practitioners already use exosome growth factors to speed up surgical recovery, but those are not autologous. Stem cells are autologous, meaning they come from the same individual: you. Because the cells are yours, they'll never be rejected by your body. They are injected beneath the skin or through an IV as a solution near an injured joint such as a bad knee. Then, they start to adapt to help repair the injury. Stem cells are effective because they go right to the place of injury and promote the recovery response.

It's possible to have your stem cells taken from fat in your body, then processed and banked. If you've had that done already, you can have your stem cells shipped to my clinic in Austin, where I can put them back into your body to enhance your recovery. (I've had mine taken and can get hold of them in 48 hours.)

The difficulties in using stem cells aren't ethical, as critics sometimes claim, but logistical. The cells must be processed in a particular way to make them usable, and the machines used to do that are expensive. Many surgical centers are nervous about investing in cutting-edge therapies that are not yet entirely accepted. However, stem-cell treatment is only going to become more popular and widespread.

I've also developed and trademarked the No-Cut Facelift, where we claim that "I can change how your face ages forever." My procedure uses heat and radiofrequency on the skin to improve texture. Skin texture is part of the rejuvenation process that traditional facelifts usually ignore. Using my therapy, it is also possible to increase the thickness of the skin, which helps avoid the papery quality that old faces sometimes have.

If you visit a cosmetic surgeon's office to talk about a facelift and all they can tell you about is Botox, a laser, or threading, you should turn around and leave. They are not interested in taking care of you, just in taking your money. They haven't looked at the available technology and are unwilling to educate themselves about how facelift procedures are improving worldwide. They've stopped being curious about getting better outcomes for patients.

## Mindset

Choosing to have surgery is a significant life decision that causes stress—but any surgeon will have more difficulty caring for a patient who is stressed. Stress makes everything more complex, so it's essential to destress yourself before surgery. Some promising research into this is exploring the effects of vagus nerve stimulation. This uses sound therapy to stimulate the two vagus nerves—one on either side of the neck—that join the lower part of our brains to the chest and stomach. The procedure seems to help get people into a parasympathetic state where their bodies are relaxed rather than stressed. As we've seen, that helps kick-start recovery even before the procedure begins.

This book is another contribution to getting a patient calm before treatment. I've written it to give you more information. That helps remove many of the unknowns that worry patients before a procedure. It's intended to reassure you about what will happen during the treatment and why so that nothing takes you by surprise.

## Biometrics

One of the potentially influential trends already happening in medicine and recovery is the rise in biometrics. A vast industry has emerged offering wearable technology that monitors vital indicators of health and recovery, from the (relatively basic) fitness tracker with most smartphones that monitor your daily steps, heart rate, and length of sleep to more sophisticated devices such as my Whoop strap. Whoop sets the standard for recovery because it monitors sleep quality, resting heart rate, heart rate variability (HRV), and other metrics. It measures strain by indicating how hard your heart works to reveal physical and mental stress.

Another leader in providing valuable metrics for predicting and monitoring recovery is the Ultrahuman Ring AIR, a titanium ring that fits on your forefinger that's so light it's very comfortable to wear. Again, it measures sleep quality, HRV, movement, and temperature, providing information that can help tweak your health. Ultrahuman also offers options to measure markers in the blood and in your daily environment that might impact your health.

Energy4Life, a company founded by Harry Massey, produces a device that studies the shape of your pulse to understand the energy flowing through the body's meridians, a feature of traditional Chinese medicine. Your pulse allows the Gem device to measure your energy and emotions because your physical shape is closely linked to your emotional health. For example, frustration is related to blocked liver energy, indicated by a wiry pulse. The Gem can then send biometric signals to your body to help correct emotional imbalances. Energy4Life also manufactures a unique light bed that works on the energy fields in the body's cells to restore your energy.

I mentioned earlier that I'm also working with a new laboratory called NVISN Labs (https://www.nvisnlabs.com), which combines genetics with drug testing so people can discover how their body metabolizes opioids and any other medications they may be taking. Those results become part of the strategic, holistic, accelerated recovery program (SHARP). It gives us even more genetic detail about you than before—before you come to the clinic or without having to leave it. Even people who aren't my patients can set up links with Nvision and submit samples from around the world for testing.

## The Future of Recovery

My approach to plastic surgery and recovery is spreading. I'm helping practices and surgeons to appreciate the role of genetics in the whole recovery program. Even more traditional surgeons who are mainly interested in being in the operating room will have support staff fully trained to prepare patients for treatment and recovery by working on their genetic profile, toxicity, nutrition, gut microbiome, and hormones.

I'm currently in the advanced planning stage of building several centers around the country and overseas dedicated to my SHARP process. I believe they will set a benchmark for cosmetic surgery in the future. They are being built around my belief that nine-tenths of the battle for having a good recovery is getting the patient in the right mindset before the treatment: relaxed and empowered rather than anxious and stressed.

Imagine the luxury of a six-star resort based on the spa hotels grand Europeans used to visit on Lake Geneva or the Cote d'Azur. After your treatment, you wake up in one of the operating rooms in the surgery center and walk - my patients can walk as soon as they wake up - directly into your private suite. You don't have to interact with anyone apart from staff trained to be empathetic to the specific needs of post-treatment patients. If you want to venture a little farther, there's a pool with space to hang out, or you can explore the enormous greenhouse buzzing with bees. You can smell the rich soil and the leaves of the organic vegetables and fruit growing around you. Then, you can enjoy the same food, prepared by talented chefs, in the commercial-grade farm-to-table kitchen.

The sustainable building will give my patients the best environment to benefit their natural recovery. Patients can relax without thinking about their diet or supplements, which are all taken care of. They can sleep well, breathe filtered air, and drink purified water. Everything will be customized to maximize the speed of each patient's recovery.

The new facilities aren't ready yet, but that doesn't mean you have to wait. Now you've discovered the surgical recovery program and the science behind it, you can start benefiting straight away.

So, put down the book and start adopting some of its practices. And let's get you a headstart on the road to recovery.

# APPENDIX

## Peptides

Peptides are a series of amino acids joined together through specific bonds. They serve essential functions in some of your body's most important and necessary processes. I don't prescribe them for various practical reasons, but if you want to know more about them, this is a summary of five of the better known peptides and their benefits.

Be aware: using peptides comes with side effects. If in doubt, consult a medical practitioner.

### PEPTIDES

ANIRACETAM (NURTURE INNER GENIUS)

Aniracetam elevates energy levels, uplifts mood through serotonin modulation, and boosts acetylcholine activity to facilitate learning, thereby enhancing cognitive function, memory, and sleep patterns. It also facilitates dopamine and serotonin interactions, boosting mood, and increases ATP levels

5-AMINO-1-MQ (ENERGY & MITOCHONDRIAL BOOST)

5-amino-1-MQ inhibits the NNMT fat-storing pathway, shrinking fat cells and deposits, and decreases the risks of diabetes, atherosclerosis, kidney, liver, and cardiovascular disease by reducing cholesterol levels by 30% over 16 weeks. 5-amino-1-MQ targets the GLUT4 pathways to improve glucose metabolism, especially when paired with exercise.

ARA 290 (PAIN RELIEF & REGENERATION)

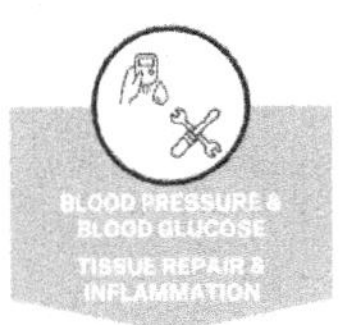


ARA 290 reduces inflammation by inhibiting cytokines IL-6, IL-12, and TNF-alpha, enhancing wound healing and tissue repair. ARA 290 stimulates blood vessel growth, stabilizes blood pressure, and reduces neuropathic pain by calming nerves and improving pain thresholds. This multifaceted peptide offers promise for addressing both vascular dysfunction and neuropathic pain.

# PEPTIDES

## EPITALON (HPA STRESS SUPPORT)

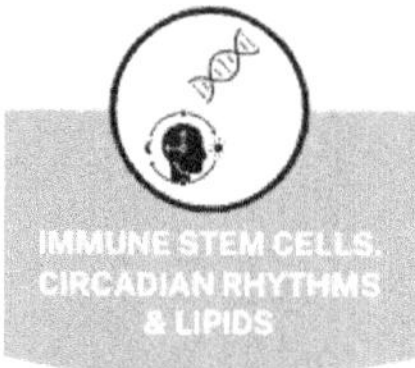


Epitalon activates telomerase activity for longevity and promotes immune stem cell differentiation by interacting with CD5. Epitalon regulates circadian rhythms and blood lipid levels by activating the pCREB and alkyamine-n-acetyltransferase pathways, which stimulate melatonin production. This dual action supports overall health by promoting a balanced sleep-wake cycle.

## GONADARELIN + KISSPEPTIN (HORMONAL HEALTH BOOST)

Kisspeptin and Gonadorelin stimulate the release of follicle-stimulating hormone (FSH) and luteinizing hormone (LH), which naturally balances hormone levels and optimizes testosterone production. By regulating these key hormones, they enhance reproductive function, support fertility, and help maintain overall hormonal equilibrium, crucial for both physical and emotional well-being.

Made in the USA
Coppell, TX
19 February 2026